"Debbie Lindell shares from the depth of her big, beautiful heart that has been nurtured and strengthened in her relationship with God and his Word. She shares from a place of brave vulnerability as she engages readers, inviting them to open themselves up to the life God has magnificently created for them to live."

—**Helen Burns**, pastor of Relate Church, author, international speaker, and cohost of *Relate with John & Helen*

"Some of the greatest joys in my life are the deep friendships I treasure with other women. They have made my life rich and strong. Debbie is one of those women. She has a profound understanding of the heart of our Father and the call on every daughter to rise up and believe what God says about who we are."

—**Sheila Walsh**, author of *The Longing in Me*

"Debbie is the real deal. She is passionate and full of grace, and she embodies a steely strength in her resolve to empower and encourage women to be all God has designed them to be. When you read this book, you will get an insight not only into Debbie's heart but also into God's divine purpose for women all across the earth. If you have ever wondered what your unique purpose was or why God would decide to use someone like you . . . this book is for you!"

—**Julia A'Bell**, lead pastor of Hillsong Church, Australia

"We first met thirteen years ago. I had just finished preaching at the Colour Conference in Sydney when a lady ran up from the back of the arena and threw her arms around me. With her heart pounding and tears flowing, she stumbled out the words, 'You have to come to Missouri.' I didn't know how to respond, but in the moment I knew my answer would be yes. That was my first encounter and the start of a God connection with my friend Debbie. Over the past thirteen years I have watched and walked with Debbie as she has lived out the words on these pages. She has dared to believe in herself, believe in her dream, and believe in countless others on the way. This book will inspire you to stop settling and start moving from where you are to where your believing heart wants to lead you. Well done, Debbie. Your courage inspires and your joy is infectious."

—**Charlotte Gambill**, lead pastor of LIFE Church UK, international speaker, and author

"Because Debbie is one of my closest friends, I have had the great God-given privilege of watching her face some of life's most difficult challenges with great faith, courage, and a lot of tears! You will laugh, you will cry, and you will totally relate to this amazing and transparent servant as she shares a bit of her journey to inspire you in your own. I cannot think of another person on the planet who is more passionate than Debbie Lindell about seeing women of all ages embrace and experience the life they were designed to live."

—**Nancy Alcorn**, founder and president of Mercy Multiplied

# She Believes

EMBRACING THE LIFE
YOU WERE
**CREATED TO LIVE**

## Debbie Lindell

WITH SUSY FLORY

Revell

a division of Baker Publishing Group
Grand Rapids, Michigan

Published by Revell
a division of Baker Publishing Group
P.O. Box 6287, Grand Rapids, MI 49516-6287
www.revellbooks.com

Printed in the United States of America

Library of Congress Cataloging-in-Publication Data
Names: Lindell, Debbie, author.
Title: She believes : embracing the life you were created to live / Debbie Lindell, with Susy Flory.
Description: Grand Rapids : Revell, 2016. | Includes bibliographical references.
Identifiers: LCCN 2016013495 | ISBN 9780800728144 (cloth) | ISBN 9780800724429 (pbk.)
Subjects: LCSH: Women—Religious aspects—Christianity. | Self-perception in women—Religious aspects. | Self-perception—Religious aspects—Christianity. | Christian women—Religious life.
Classification: LCC BT704 .L56 2016 | DDC 248.8/43—dc23
LC record available at https://lccn.loc.gov/2016013495

All images are copyright and used courtesy of James River Church.

Some names and details have been changed to protect the privacy of the individuals involved.

Author is represented by the literary agency of Alive Communications, Inc., 7680 Goddard Street, Suite 200, Colorado Springs, CO 80920, www.alivecommunications.com.

16   17   18   19   20   21   22      7   6   5   4   3   2   1

To my Heavenly Father.
Believing in you and what you say about me
changed everything about my life.

# CONTENTS

## Section 1: Believing . . . You Were Designed on Purpose

*Open up before God, keep nothing back; he'll do whatever needs to
be done: He'll validate your life in the clear light of day and stamp you
with approval at high noon. (Ps. 37:5-6)*

## Section 2: Believing . . . Changes Your Heart

*You're blessed when you get your inside world—your mind and
heart—put right. (Matt. 5:8)*

Contents

# FOREWORD

There is nothing like that moment when a woman is awakened to the truth that she is who God says she is, she can do what God says she can do, and she can have all that God says she can have.

That moment when her faith makes the six-inch drop from her head to her heart, and her passion, purpose, and potential are activated.

That is the moment when everything changes.

Forever.

Great power is unleashed when you are no longer paralyzed by fear, doubt, unbelief, or insecurity and are instead fueled by faith and trust in an awesome God.

There is no stopping a woman who believes God.

You are here on purpose for a purpose.

You matter very much.

The earth awaits your contribution.

This is not a dress rehearsal.

You only have one life—make it count.

It is not too late to start believing God.

You are not hopeless, useless, insignificant, irrelevant, or a failure.

Nothing that has been said or done to you or against you is greater than what Jesus has done for you.

Your limitations are not greater than God's supernatural ability to work through you.

There is more in you than you know.

You are enough.

He is more than enough.

My friend Debbie lives the message of this book. I have watched her grow, thrive, and flourish as she passionately embraced the journey, struggle, and change required to become a woman who truly *believes*. Her life is having a profound impact on multitudes, and so can yours.

Her faith, joy, and enthusiasm inspire me, and I know they will do the same for you in this book. Don't just casually flip through these pages; write all over them and apply them, and you will find yourself living a life that you once only dreamed about.

"Now to him who is able to do immeasurably more than all we ask or imagine, according to his power that is at work within us" (Eph. 3:20 NIV).

Christine Caine
Founder, Propel Women

# ACKNOWLEDGMENTS

To the love of my life and very best friend, John. Believing God together continues to be a great adventure. Your faith inspires me, babe, and your belief in me made this book come to life. I'll love you forever!

To my ever-expanding family. You bring me so much joy! There are not enough words to describe how much I love each one of you. I am one very blessed mom!

To my amazing parents, Tim and Bonnie, for teaching me to trust God and live a joy-filled life.

To the sweetest mom-in-law ever, Eileen, for loving me like her own and leading me closer to Jesus.

To the beautiful sisterhood who surround me with friendship, love, laughter, and blessing—you were my inspiration!

To my friends in ministry, for challenging me to chase after the God dreams in my heart.

To all who supported and prayed for me through every step of this journey.

To Susy Flory, for sharing your writing wisdom. You were a gift from heaven!

To the Baker Publishing team for walking beside me with patience, kindness, and encouragement.

# INTRODUCTION
## Do You Believe What You Believe?

I am so excited to be sharing this moment in time with you, and I do not believe it is by accident that you are holding this book in your hand. I would guess you are a girl, or a woman, depending on how you look at it. Personally, I like to refer to all of us on the feminine side of God's creation as *girls*. It just sounds happy and a bit more inclusive to me. In my opinion, no matter what year you were born, whether you wear pink ruffled skirts or faded blue jeans, or if your hair is red, blonde, amber, or a gorgeous shade of gray, if you were born a baby girl, you still are every bit a girl. And I believe that the words in this book are for you!

I want you to know that I have been praying for you since the moment I began the *She Believes* journey. Praying that your life will be changed by the words inside these pages. Praying that you will be encouraged to believe things that you never dreamed possible for yourself, your relationships, your home, and your future. I definitely don't claim to have all the answers, because just like you, I am striving to learn and grow to understand who I am in Christ and all that he desires for me to believe for my life. But through my journey of learning to believe, God has put in me a desire to do everything I can to encourage girls of every age to believe too!

So let me ask you this question: What do you believe?

What do you really believe about yourself, about your life, and about your Creator? What do you believe about why you were chosen to be alive at this moment in history?

How you answer each of those questions affects how you are living your life—whether you are just surviving or whether you are living filled with joy and anticipation, trusting and believing your Heavenly Father has amazing things planned just for you each and every day.

Nearly thirteen years ago, I attended a women's conference that changed my life forever. One of the speakers who graced the stage shared a message called "Your Life Is a Gift." I'll never forget the impact of her words on my heart as she spoke about how God designed each one of us exactly how he wants us to be; all we need to do is believe that, unwrap the package of our lives, and watch God use us in ways we've never dreamed or imagined.

Something clicked inside of me that day. I could either believe that God had created me to do great things, or I could keep sitting back in the shadows of doubt and unbelief and miss out on all he had for me. I asked myself the question, Do I really believe what I believe?

Maybe you are in a place today where you are having trouble believing what you believe. That God is really there, that he knows who you are, and that he has amazing plans for your life and your future. Maybe your circumstances are screaming at you, causing you to doubt that your life has any real purpose or meaning at all. Or perhaps you feel like you're at the end of your rope, just hanging by a fraying thread of hope.

The Bible says this:

> I know the plans that I have for you, declares the Lord. They are plans for peace and not disaster, plans to give you a future filled with hope. (Jer. 29:11 GW)

Whether you are trying to understand and figure out your life; striving to be a good daughter, mom, or wife; or possibly looking at your future with doubt and uncertainty, my deepest desire is that no matter where you find yourself today, the message in this book will capture your heart and change your life. No matter what you think, no matter the circumstances you are facing, no matter what you have heard in your past or been taught to think about yourself, *you*, precious girl, were magnificently and beautifully designed for life. And when you believe that . . . *everything changes!*

Grab a cup of coffee (or whatever sounds good), and I'll meet you in chapter 1.

BELIEVING . . .

# You Were Designed on Purpose

Open up before GOD, keep nothing back;
he'll do whatever needs to be done:
He'll validate your life in the clear light of day
and stamp you with approval at high noon.
Psalm 37:5–6

# *One*

## You Are a Masterpiece

For we are God's masterpiece. He has created us.
(Eph. 2:10 NLT)

**de•signed:** intentionally planned; artistically, skillfully, and purposefully fashioned

> Life isn't about finding yourself;
> it's about understanding
> who you were created to be.

The artist and designer had been working on his project for months and planning it for more years than he could count. This magnificent work of art was his very own unique creation. It wasn't a copy of anything he had seen before. He had carefully and purposefully selected each shade of color and the exact shape and curve for every part. Each tiny, intricate detail was meticulously and perfectly designed.

As the day for the revealing came closer, he took time to add a few finishing touches, a detail here and there to set this project apart from all the others. Up until this moment, no one but him had even glimpsed the beauty of this extraordinary creation.

His masterpiece was now complete. He stepped back to gaze at what he had made and smiled to himself. *This is exactly what I envisioned. It's perfect. I absolutely love everything about it!*

He was so very proud. He couldn't wait to reveal it to the world!

———

Genesis talks about all that God created, along with his design and purpose for humanity. It tells us this in chapter 5:

This is the book (the written record, the history) of the generations of the offspring of Adam. When God created man, He made
him in the likeness of God. (v. 1 AMP-CE)

God made everything. But most importantly, for his pleasure, he
made mankind. Every human being who has ever lived and every baby
who will ever be born was and is intentionally and purposefully and
beautifully made by God to display his glory. And that includes you!

In her pitch-black cocoon, she felt safe and secure. The only
sounds were those she had heard for months now—distant, muf-
fled voices and the constant soothing sound that had become so
comforting to her. *Thump, tha-thump . . . thump, tha-thump.* She
had only one challenge. The space that had been her home was
getting rather cozy and even uncomfortable. With her arms and
legs folded tightly up against her tiny body, she was beginning to
have trouble moving. She was growing rapidly now, and it was
obvious that something was going to have to change.

Then one day, out of nowhere, she felt an odd and unfamiliar
sensation. An unexplained pressure pushed up against her, surrounding her. She did her best to ignore it and slowly drifted back
to sleep, sucking her thumb.

Her eyes fluttered open. *Now what? What is this?* The pressure
was back, and it was stronger now, making her even more uncomfortable. Forget sleeping. She was fully awake and even starting
to get a bit anxious.

*What is happening?* She could hear her own heart beating faster
as the tightening increased and her little body felt as though it was
being forced to move . . . but where?

And then, in an instant, everything changed!

The security of the only home she had ever known disappeared
in a flash, replaced by a world filled with light, cold air, noise, and

sensations she had never known before. But as her mind tried to process what was happening, she heard these three little words: "It's a girl!"

And that girl was you.

---

Do you know that you are one in a hundred million?

When you were born, the world was given an amazing gift—your life! Whether you choose to believe it or not, you are an incredible work of original art—a masterpiece. Your life is beautiful, created and designed by God, the ultimate master artist and designer. There has never been anyone like you on earth, and there will never ever be another girl born who is exactly like you.

You, gorgeous girl, are one of a kind!

I know we have just met, but I want to talk to you about sex. That's right, you read that correctly. S-E-X!

That got your attention, didn't it? I am a firm believer in having sex and lots of it. I think it is a total blast and should be for everyone (as long as you're married, that is). Well, I hate to disappoint you, but that is not the aspect of sex I want to talk about.

What I do want to talk about is how you were made, because it's pretty incredible and I think it's important for you to understand.

We all know what happens at the moment of conception. Just in case you forgot, let me remind you. Your body began to form when a single egg from your mother and one microscopic sperm from your father found each other and connected inside your mother's body.

But that is not really when your life began. Your existence was planned and purposed by your Creator long before that moment.

I want to remind you how amazing it is that you, precious girl, are here on the planet today. When you think about the odds of that one egg and one sperm coming together to create you, it is absolutely mind blowing! This thought is relevant to what you believe about yourself, how you view your Creator God, and why you are even alive today.

Listen, sweet girl, because this is really important. Your beautiful life was planned and designed long before your parents had sex and your mom became pregnant with you. And no matter how it happened—whether it was a good situation or not so good, or what the circumstances were—you were not a mistake! God wanted you to be born. He planned for you to exist, and he was over-the-moon excited about your birth.

Whether you believe in God or even question whether the Bible is true, you need to hear what I am saying, because it affects everything about how you will live your life and what you believe about yourself. The Bible says this about you:

> Long before he laid down earth's foundations, he had [you] in mind [planned for you to be born], had settled on [you] as the focus of his love. (Eph. 1:4, brackets mine)

Did you catch that? God knew who you were before you were even born. The book of Psalms says God saw your unformed body, and all the days of your life were ordained by him before one of them came to be (see Ps. 139:16).

Isn't that incredible to think about? You were not an accident or just the coincidence of two people having sex. You were planned for and wanted, created on purpose by the God of the universe. Pretty awesome!

Let's talk about sex again for a minute. There are two kinds of sperm that every male produces and emits during sex. They are called X and Y. If an X sperm fertilizes the mother's egg, a baby girl is conceived. If a Y sperm completes the job, a baby boy is conceived. Now, here is why that is important for you to know. During sex, an average of a hundred million sperm enter a woman's body. You read that right—a *hundred million!* And as they are designed to do, each one starts competing to make it to the prize first—the one lone egg tucked up inside the mother-to-be's body.

When you were conceived, one of those itsy, bitsy, tiny sperm from your father's body had to survive and swim for ten hours to find that one egg. That was one physically fit sperm!

When your mother was born, her ovaries already contained a lifetime supply of eggs. Millions and millions of little potential life makers in waiting, each one the size of a tiny grain of salt.

Now listen to this, because it is so amazing! On the day you were conceived, out of those millions of eggs inside your mother's body, just one was waiting there for the fastest-swimming sperm to find it. That one egg, like the sperm, possessed a unique combination of twenty-three chromosomes. And when it connected with that one-in-a-hundred-million sperm, together they created a brand-new, completely unique human being. You!

Of course, the mother's egg and father's sperm don't just pass along a copy of their chromosomes but rather new, unique chromosomes that contain a mixture of the genes from your parents, ensuring each new child is genetically and distinctly and altogether different from any other.

All of this miraculous coming together was preplanned and predetermined. God planned for that sperm and egg to come together to create you because he wanted you to be alive! And when he made you, he loved every single detail about you.

Here is something else the Bible says about your creation: your body was formed inside and out by God. That means every intricate part of your being, from the top of your head to the tip of your toes, was meticulously put together by his hands. You are his very own handiwork, his workmanship, created to be on the earth at this moment in time. You, precious girl, were perfectly, magnificently, and beautifully designed to be alive today!

You were perfectly created by the God of the universe.

By the One who made the sun rise up in the sky this morning.

By the One who created every star and calls each one of them by name.

By the One who made every plant, tree, and flower.

By the One who designed the mountains and oceans and every amazing creature that lives.

He, your Heavenly Father, brought all the details together to make your life happen. Why?

Well, the truth is, just because he wanted to. He wanted you to be a part of his plan for this moment in time. He anticipated the day of your birth. He knew your name before you were born, and he was completely prepared to welcome this brand-new baby girl into the world.

---

Our daughter Savannah's conception was a huge surprise. Even though God knew she was going to be in our family, we were not expecting her to come when she did. Now, you would have thought that since we already had two little boys—David and Brandon, who were under the age of two—we would have understood the potential consequences of having sex (there's that word again!). But no, we did not seem to take notice of the fact that I was extremely fertile. It seemed as though I could get pregnant just by looking at John. So within six months of giving birth to our second son, Savannah was conceived, to my shock, fear, and denial. Soon (in nine months, to be exact) we would have three children in diapers, and none of them would be able to communicate in full sentences. This was going to be interesting!

The morning Savannah was born, I remember waking up with a jolt. My due date was still almost two weeks away. It looked like this little sister was not going to reach her due date, just as her brothers hadn't. I quietly slipped out of bed, got dressed, did a five-minute makeup job (because a girl's got to have makeup on during labor and delivery), and went back into our bedroom to wake up John.

"Hey, babe. Wake up. Today you're going to become a daddy of a baby girl."

*A baby girl . . .* Just saying it made me smile.

John and I made it to the hospital just in time. We went in at 7:30 a.m., and she was in my arms by 9:35 a.m. Love those quick babies! I remember looking at her very wiggly little body and realizing from the moment she appeared, she was nothing like the boys. First of all, she was so tiny, barely six pounds. But besides her weight, she was just different. Her face had petite, feminine features, and her tiny, delicate fingers looked nothing like the chunky, stubby fingers of her brothers. Then there was her anatomy. She was in every way a girl! One of John's X sperm had won my prize egg—the egg with the chromosomes needed to create this little baby girl with olive skin, dark hair, little rosebud lips, and a very loud, screechy cry!

At first, when they brought her to me, I actually wondered if she was really our baby. Her skin was so dark, and her little round head was covered with wispy, nearly black hair. But since she was the only baby girl in our small-town hospital that day, she was the only option. She was ours!

The nurse came in to fill out some paperwork. "What is the baby's name?" she asked.

"We don't know yet," I said, gazing down at my daughter's sweet face. For the next three days, everyone called her Baby Girl Lindell because her mom and dad weren't ready to give her a name. I know that's terrible, but we have a good excuse: we were sleep-deprived parents. Neither of her brothers were sleeping through the night yet. They were both up several times a night. Every night! We had tried every "how to make your baby sleep" book out there, even hanging Christmas lights and playing music. Nothing worked. So I just don't think we'd had the energy or mental capacity to make such an important decision, at least not yet. We were too tired.

The morning we were scheduled to be dismissed from the hospital, a nurse walked into my room and informed us emphatically that we had to give our baby a name before we could leave. Thankfully by then we had narrowed down our options: Stephanie, Sheri, Scarlet, Savannah, and Olivia. John was leaning toward one name, while I liked them all. How about Stephanie Sheri Scarlet Savannah Olivia Lindell?

I don't recall how we finally made the decision, but for our daughter's sake we managed to pick one name. And with that, her proud-as-punch mom and dad took Savannah Marie Lindell home. But poor girl, naming her was not the only thing we weren't prepared for. She didn't have a bedroom either. We lived in a tiny, two-bedroom house. Savannah's two older brothers and their cribs took up the small second bedroom across the hall from ours. So when she grew out of the little cradle beside our bed, the only place for her to go was on the lime-green, floral, hand-me-down loveseat in the living room. For the next six months of her life, the living room was Savannah's bedroom.

But even though she was a surprise to us, and even though we as parents weren't ready for her arrival and didn't even have a name picked out for her, God was fully prepared for her birth. He had been expecting her to come on her birthday since the beginning of time!

And it's the same with you. He not only was fully prepared for you, and he not only knew your name (even if your parents didn't), but everything about you was perfect to him. From the very moment you were born, you brought him joy!

Listen to this:

> You go before me and follow me.
>   You place your hand of blessing on my head.
> Such knowledge is too wonderful for me,
>   too great for me to understand! . . .
> How precious are your thoughts about me, O God.
>   (Ps. 139:5–6, 17 NLT)

On the day you showed up on the planet and the words "It's a girl" announced your birth, God celebrated you because you were exactly who you were made to be—a beautiful and magnificently designed masterpiece. And he was thrilled out of his mind to reveal you for the world to see.

"Look at her. I made her—isn't she absolutely beautiful!"

Yes, you are!

*Two*

# Your Reflection Is Beautiful

Do you not know that your body is the temple (the very sanctuary) of the Holy Spirit Who lives within you, Whom you have received [as a Gift] from God? You are not your own, you were bought with a price. . . . So then, honor God and bring glory to Him in your body. (1 Cor. 6:19–20 AMP-CE)

**unique:** one of a kind, unlike anyone else

**beau•ti•ful:** having qualities that bring joy and delight

The things that make you different
are the things that make you beautiful.

was very nervous. *What will he think of us? What will he think of me?*

John and I were about to sit through our first job interview as a married couple. We were early, and as we sat side by side in a booth in the corner of a restaurant, my stomach felt like it was in one big knot. We were both twenty-one years old and had been married only a year. It didn't feel to me like we were quite ready for this next step in life.

When the pastor arrived in his suit and tie, he looked taller than I had remembered. He greeted us warmly and sat down across the table from us. We were both anxious and excited as we started the interview for our first ministry position. If we were hired, we would be working under this man at a prominent church in our community.

I wondered, *Am I dressed right?* John looked so sharp in his dress pants and button-down shirt. I was so proud as I watched him answer each question with confidence and assurance. I don't remember saying much, if anything, as the pastor's eyes and attention seemed exclusively fixed on John. He was listening intently as John answered his questions and shared his views on leadership and ministry. It didn't matter to me, as I really didn't care to talk. Instead, I preferred to stay quiet and hope that I wouldn't say or do anything that would mess up our prospects of being hired for the position.

Finally, after an hour or so, as the interview was coming to a close, the pastor glanced at me briefly and then looked back at John. With his deep, radio-style voice that seemed to command the attention of the entire restaurant, he said, "Well, John . . ." He stopped a moment to clear his throat. "I can see that you are a very gifted young man. And on a scale of one to ten, I would most definitely rate you at a ten." He paused again and turned back to look at me. "But your wife—I would only rate her at a four."

My breath caught in my chest as my mind processed what he was saying.

Then he added to clarify, "She will be your liability."

As his words worked their way down into my heart and soul, I felt as if every one of my glaring faults and inadequacies had been exposed, even though I'd tried my best to cover them up. I thought about how easily this pastor had assessed that I didn't have much to offer. What I feared most—holding John back from going where he could go in the ministry—was already coming to pass and affecting an opportunity for him. In that moment, as I fought to keep the tears gathering in my eyes from dripping down my face, I felt John's big, strong hand on my knee, gently and reas-suringly giving it a squeeze under the table. I knew he was doing his best to support and encourage me. But it was too late. The pastor's assessment had confirmed all that I had come to believe about myself, and I was sure that he was right.

Somehow between the day I had taken my first breath and the day I sat there hearing this man's assessment of me, I had bought into believing the lie that I, Deborah Joy Lindell, was a deficient creation. A faulty design.

Since grade school I'd struggled with accepting and believing in myself, and now that challenge had followed me into my adult-hood. Not only did I struggle with the idea that my personality was deficient and inadequate for church ministry, but I was also convinced my body shape and appearance were lacking in multiple areas too. I was small in places where I thought I should be big (you can probably guess where—my boobs, for one!). And I was big in places where I thought I should be small, like my nose and my ankles. My teeth were crooked, my toes were stubby, my legs weren't slender, and my hair . . . well, what do you do with hair that doesn't seem to know if it is curly or straight? Clearly something must have gone wrong when I was being designed.

*Perhaps God was distracted and made mistakes when he created me, or maybe he just selected me not to be designed as perfectly and beautifully as other girls.*

The truth was, in almost every way I didn't feel like I matched up to girls around me in regards to talent, looks, intelligence, or personality.

My body. I definitely felt like it had issues. For one thing, ever since I was in junior high, when I looked at my face in the mirror, all I could see was my nose. I had come to hate looking at it. It was much too wide, and over the years people had confirmed what I feared was true. My nose was one of the obvious errors in the design of my face. I tried clothespins to fix the issue, just like Amy in *Little Women*. That remedy proved to be very painful and not at all effective. I tried makeup tricks, like using a dark brown eye pencil to draw a line down each side of my nose, with a dab of highlighter on the tip and a stripe down the middle, to give an illusion of a thin, more perfectly shaped nose. It didn't seem to make much of a difference.

Then there was my chest. Up until I was an adult, it hardly mattered if I wore a bra or not. I tried creative home remedies for that issue too. But when a wad of toilet paper came waving out of my shirt in English class, I knew that was not going to work long term! God had definitely made an error on that part too. But how could he? Didn't he know that a girl needed boobs bigger than four cotton balls?

Along with my body design issues, there were deficiencies with my talents, abilities, and personality type. I was shy, but I could talk and laugh too much (go figure). I was unorganized and flighty. I wasn't at all gifted in athletics, but I was very competitive (now that's an interesting combination). I wasn't especially intelligent but was very outspoken. What a messy, mixed-up, crazy, unproductive combination I seemed to be. What in the world was God thinking?

As a young adult, I tried taking different personality tests to see if I could fix myself. But whenever I got the results, I was disappointed. I so desperately wanted to be something other than what the tests showed—a laid-back, messy person with more than one junk drawer to my name. I wanted to be naturally neat, organized, and disciplined. I wanted to journal every day and read my Bible through once a year. I wanted to color inside the lines and say just the right thing every time I opened my mouth. But no matter how hard I tried or what test I took, I didn't have a place for everything and everything wasn't in its place. I wasn't consistent and steady. And way too often I embarrassed myself when I talked too much and tried to be the life of the party.

What I feared most always seemed to be confirmed. I was not what I wanted to be, and I was not the best and most beautiful design.

My insecurities and low self-worth were not a result of any abuse or harsh treatment as a child. I wasn't exposed to unkind words or blatant media lies that would have tainted my view of myself. I was blessed with a healthy, loving home where I was protected, nurtured, and cared for. But in spite of that, I still found myself in a battle for value and worth that, if left unchecked and unchallenged, would completely debilitate the life God intended me to live. What I didn't understand that day in the restaurant, and what that well-meaning but obviously uninformed pastor did not understand either, is that one of Satan's most destructive and effective tools is to cause girls to doubt their worth and value. The enemy wants to make us believe we are flawed and less than beautifully designed by our Creator.

It's highly likely that you can relate in some way to my story. If you are one of the nine out of ten women or girls who struggle with low self-worth, you have battled similar thoughts and feelings about yourself at some point in your life. And it is possible that you still do.

We don't necessarily think of everyday, well-adjusted girls—meaning those who seem confident on the outside—as struggling with self-worth. But the truth of the matter is that low self-esteem is not deterred by race, social class, or age group, nor does it affect only a specific kind of woman with a certain type of background. Even a woman or girl who looks like she has it all together on the outside has most likely struggled with her self-worth.

In a study conducted at the New York University Child Study Center, Dr. Robin F. Goodman discovered that "girls' self-esteem peaks when they are nine years old, then takes a nose dive."[1] The same study also reported that 75 percent of eight- and nine-year-olds like their looks, but that figure drops to 56 percent once girls reach ages twelve and thirteen. That is a very sad statistic! Nearly one out of every two girls (and probably women too) struggle with who they are.

What I have come to understand over my years of working with girls of every age, shape, and size is that nearly every one of them, at some point, has battled the lie that her body and personality are deficient in some way. It is obvious to me that Satan wants each one of us to feel insufficient, and he will do whatever he can to keep us from understanding and believing that we are in every way uniquely, perfectly, and beautifully designed by God. And he never ever stops trying to get us to believe that lie. Instead, he takes every opportunity possible to keep us from believing the truth. It doesn't matter what your upbringing was like; he will do whatever he can to distort and disfigure and taint your view of who God created you to be and, in doing so, affect your view of God.

He will do it by any means possible—through the words and views of others, through inaccurate biblical teaching, through media messaging, or through thoughts and feelings that are not in line with God's truth. And as he accomplishes his devious and destructive work, you find yourself believing something much less than the truth.

That is exactly what happened to a precious and beautiful girl named Sherry. She too was raised in a healthy, happy home where she was loved and cared for by her parents. But in spite of that, she never fully understood that the Creator designed her uniquely, perfectly, and beautifully. She is eighty years old now, and for the past forty years of her life, she has been confined to the inside of her home. Not because someone locked her in the house but because she locked herself in, using the keys of her own insecurities. She is so afraid that people, including her own sister, will see her imperfections that she made the choice to hide from the pain of being discovered. Not only has she been robbed of happiness and joy, but the world has been shortchanged too, missing out on everything her amazing life had to offer.

The lie of "not good enough" is one that has no boundaries. It's a lie that labors endlessly to weave its way into your heart and mind through the words you hear, the messages you see, and even your inner human nature, constantly inviting you to compare yourself to others. This lie works tirelessly to destroy the truth of God's Word and the magnificent creation he fashioned you to be.

God says this about you: Your body is absolutely beautiful! Your mind is altogether amazing! And your personality and talents were perfectly chosen to make you who you are!

I honestly believe these words could change your life . . . because they changed mine!

In Psalm 139:13–14, David writes this as he gives praise to God about his own body and design:

> You made all the delicate, inner parts of my body
> and knit me together in my mother's womb.
> Thank you for making me so wonderfully complex!
> Your workmanship is marvelous—how well I know it.
> (NLT)

The man who wrote those words was not some manic, narcissistic person filled with self-love and pride. The Bible actually describes him as a man after the heart of God. This guy loved God deeply and wanted to honor him with his life and words. Through God's leading, he sets an example in those words of how we should view and speak about the design and creation of our mind and body.

Here's the deal. When you do not believe the truth about who God created you to be, and when you do not respect, honor, and give glory to him for what he has made (and that includes yourself and your body), you dishonor, disrespect, and discredit his creation. Seriously!

When I came to the realization that the view I had of myself revealed a lack of faith and trust in God's words about me, when I understood that I was not honoring him with the thoughts and words I had about myself, and when I humbly asked for his forgiveness and his grace to see myself through his eyes, it changed me. I no longer focused my attention on myself and on my distorted view of my body, abilities, and personality. By being confident in the fact that God made me exactly how he wanted me to be, I could focus on others and give God the praise and honor he deserved.

Ephesians 1:11–12 tells us that it is only through our understanding of how God views us, and through believing in him and his love for us, that we can fully comprehend who we were created to be.

It's in Christ that we find out who we are and what we are living for. Long before we first heard of Christ and got our hopes up, he had his eye on us, had designs on us for glorious living, part of the overall purpose he is working out in everything and everyone.

The Word of God teaches us not only about life but also about who we are and what he has created us to be. God is shouting out to you and every girl, "I *love* you, I *created* you, and I have a *purpose* for you!"

Believing God intended to create you just the way you are is one of the most important faith decisions you will ever make. And the sooner you accept who you were designed to be, the sooner you will move toward freedom from insecurity and to an understanding of God's plan and purpose for your life.

This is truly one of my greatest passions in life—to see girls set free from this lie of Satan. And it is my prayer that if you are trapped in the bondage of insecurity and low self-worth, you will listen to these words and begin to understand who you were made to be. That you will be free to honor and praise God for his incredible creation . . . YOU! It is then that you will be able to radiantly reflect the beauty of your Creator to the world through your personality, your body, and your beautiful life!

Sometime today I want you to stand in front of a full-length mirror. Look at yourself. Don't inspect or tear down what you see. Just stop and thank God for what he made. You can start with the words in this prayer. It might be difficult at first, but it is the right thing to do, because as you praise God for what you see, you will be giving him glory for what he made when he made you!

*Dear Heavenly Father,*
*Thank you for perfectly and uniquely designing me.*
*Thank you for making me just the way I am, from the color of my hair to the toenails on my feet. Thank you for my body.*

*Thank you for creating my mind and giving me the personality and abilities that you want me to have. I praise you because I was created in your image and by your design. You made me beautiful in every way!*

*Help me to always give you the glory and honor you deserve and to believe that what you made me to be is perfect and beautiful, because you created me to glorify you.*

*Amen.*

You might just be wondering what happened with our job interview at the restaurant. In spite of his negative thoughts and opinions about my abilities, surprisingly the pastor offered us a position on his staff. John and I took some time to pray about it, and we both agreed that we should accept the position. We served under that pastor's leadership for nearly two years. It wasn't the easiest season in our lives, but through that time we learned how to work and serve under those who didn't see life or people exactly the way we did. We also learned much about the ministry and how to lead, strengthen, and encourage people to be all God created them to be.

Looking back, I am thankful for the experience, because more than anything it taught me what it feels like to have someone not believe in you. I realized that my worth and value come from God, who designed and created me just the way he wanted me to be. And that is one of the most valuable lessons I have ever learned!

# *Three*

## Your Story Matters

Write this down for the next generation
    so people not yet born will praise God. . . .
Write it so the story can be told in Zion,
    so God's praise will be sung.

Psalm 102:18, 21

**sto•ry:** a recounting of events that have already happened, preserving a picture of the past and setting the stage for the future

In every ordinary life, there is
an extraordinary story waiting to be told.

Do you remember the last time you read a novel or story about someone and it mesmerized your thoughts, keeping you glued to every word? Do you remember the excitement of turning each page, your mind filled with anticipation because you couldn't wait to see what was going to happen next? You were captivated by the story.

Every girl's life is a story that is unique to her. The people connected to her past, the places she has been, and the events she has walked through all intertwine to display the person she is today. Your story is no different. It is being written using words from your past and formed by the stories of those who have lived before you. No story is the same, but every story is precious and treasured by God. He loves history, and he loves your history. Why? Because it is what makes you who you are. It is literally your lifeline. What I want you to know from the beginning of this chapter is that although your history is what has brought you to this moment in time, it does not define who you will be tomorrow. You, precious girl, determine that!

My history may not seem that remarkable to some, but it is to me. It is my life. Just like yours, it has imperfections, but it reveals this truth—that Jesus can take the broken parts of any story and make them whole by his grace.

I am a northern girl at the core. I love snow! Maybe that has something to do with being born in the heart of Minneapolis. My mother, Yvonne Arleen (nicknamed Bonnie at birth), was born just up the road from there, in the not-so-well-known town of Two Harbors, twenty-four years before me. She is beautiful in every way, a strong but gentle person with a quick smile and sweet disposition. She is hardworking and to this day has stamina beyond her years. She has always been an incredible homemaker and loves to make her house look like a fairy-tale cottage for anyone and everyone who comes inside. Without even breaking a sweat, Mom can sew and bake (at the same time) and pretty much do anything she sets her mind to. She rarely sits still. And on top of all that, she loves God with all her heart. She, more than anyone, taught me what a godly, hardworking, servant-hearted woman looks like.

My dad, Tim, is one of the most amazing men I've ever known. In spite of his sometimes sad, disappointing, and tumultuous growing-up years and the absence of any stability in his life, he has been a wonderful father to me. He has been a dedicated husband to my mom and a faithful father to our family for over fifty years. Most importantly, he is passionate about using every part of his life to honor God, and I grew up observing that desire in all he did. Now, when I was a child, my family wasn't rich, and we had challenging times for sure, but with two loving parents who were committed to honoring God, I had a childhood filled with wonderful memories—laughter, hugs, good food, playing all sorts of games, and fishing (I can put a worm on a hook like the best of them).

My mom was born to some of the most precious people I have ever known—my grandparents Obed and Alice Balken. Although I think they were very special, they were not perfect. Their lives together as a couple started out with a huge challenge when, to their dismay, they found themselves expecting a child four months before they were to be married. In spite of this disappointment (with themselves more than anything), they chose to look to God and believe he could still use them. I'm sure that took faith! In those days, sadly, you kept that kind of "mistake" a secret . . . hopefully forever. Thankfully they decided to still get married, and soon they found themselves pastoring a tiny church in the little town of Two Harbors with their baby girl.

Within three years, two sons were added to their home, and not long after that, their youngest was born—my mom. When she was five years old, the family moved to the city of Minneapolis. It was there that my mom grew up in a tiny white house attached to the little church my grandparents pastored for thirty-two years.

My dad's history is much different. He was born two years after my mom, thousands of miles from Minnesota, in Spokane, Washington. The circumstances of his conception would not belong in a fairy tale, nor would anyone choose them to be a part of their history. His mother, an unassuming, quiet teenage girl, was staying at the home of some friends for the summer when a teenage boy raped her and she became pregnant.

I've known this story for years, but for some reason, as I share it with you today, it's making me emotional. My grandmother's rape is a part of who I am; it is my history. It's both difficult and incredible to comprehend that in the midst of horrendous and unwanted circumstances, my father's life began. I can't begin to imagine how my grandmother must have felt as her assailant walked away, leaving her lying there in pain and shame. She had no idea that in those few dreadful moments, a new life was created that would later create mine.

Because of how people in those days viewed a pregnant, unmarried girl, my grandmother tried desperately to hide the situation from the world around her. She was certain no one in the small and very connected community would ever believe her story. She knew the boy—he went to church with her. So to escape the shame, she left and went alone into hiding, where she gave birth to my dad, a curly-haired, blond baby she named Timothy.

Thinking there was only one option, she made the decision to give her son up for adoption to a family she hoped would care and provide for him better than she could. But it didn't work out that way.

My dad's new home was a very dysfunctional one. His adoptive mother tried to hold the family together, but within a few years, her husband abandoned them and she was left to raise my dad on her own. With her life spiraling out of control, she moved to Seattle with her young son to live with her aging mother. For the next few years, between the ages of eight and ten, my dad was basically left to fend for himself, selling newspapers on the streets of the town to make money to live on.

His life at that point went from bad to worse. On two separate occasions, he was raped by men who threatened to hurt him if he told anyone. Somehow my dad was brave enough to tell his mom, and that is when she decided to put him in boarding school to get him off the street. It was there that he spent the next seven years away from the only family he had known. During all those years, his mother came to visit him only two times, and the day he graduated from high school, not one person was there to celebrate with him.

Here is the part about my dad's story that I want you to hear. One day, back when he was just seven years old, in the middle of all that heartache, he went to a church service with his grandmother and heard about Jesus. He told me, "Debbie Joy, that was the day my life was changed. I asked Jesus to come into my heart. And do you know what? When I went back home to the same sad house, everything was different. It felt like the trees were clapping their hands with joy."

God loved my dad and was there to help him when he looked to him. This reminds me of the story of Joseph in the book of Genesis. Joseph's story was very much like my father's in that it was filled with disappointment and heartache. He was abandoned by his family, left to die, forced into slavery, lied about, and severely mistreated. But in the midst of the broken pieces in Joseph's life, God was working behind the scenes to weave together a story that would display his grace and forgiveness to the world. And in the end Joseph said, "What was meant for evil, God turned around for good!" (see Gen. 50:20).

Similarly, in spite of all the heartache, turmoil, and loneliness that were a part of his childhood, my dad found Jesus and never looked back.

Then, through a series of crazy and unexpected events (you will just have to believe me on that), this twenty-two-year-old from Seattle, with his very dysfunctional past, just happened to meet a shy pastor's daughter from Minnesota.

And they fell in love and got married.

How do these things happen? Only God!

My parents didn't have much their first few years of marriage. Actually, they didn't have a thing. For over a year, they lived with my grandparents in their little house attached to the church. And within a month of their wedding day, I was conceived. My eyes are tearing up as I think about how God brought my parents together—two very different people from two very different backgrounds—to create my life. When I was born, I was a scrawny little thing weighing in at a whopping five pounds, four ounces. But I was a new life—a life that from the beginning of time God had purposed to be born on July 9 at 9:15 a.m.

How did it happen? Simply put, he wanted me, Deborah Joy Keene Lindell, to be a part of his story. Me, this complex yet simple human being, woven together from the bits and pieces of my parents, my grandparents, and their stories before mine. The same is true for you. The very moment you were born, whether it was fifteen or ninety years ago, your heaven-planned story began.

*Your story may not seem like a big deal to you, but it is a big deal to God.*

Your story matters.

Listen to what Psalm 18 says:

> GOD made my life complete
>> when I placed all the pieces before him.
> When I got my act together,
>> he gave me a fresh start. . . .
> GOD rewrote the text of my life
>> when I opened the book of my heart to his eyes.
>> (vv. 20–21, 24)

You, my friend, are a beautiful book in the making. Yes, it is true that your history has been sealed in chapters already written. You cannot go back and change what has happened. They are pages for the record books, sprinkled with memories, some that are cherished and others that may bring tears of pain and regret. But every part is known to God, and he can take each one and create a story that reveals grace and beauty.

> It stands to reason, doesn't it, that if the alive-and-present God who raised Jesus from the dead moves into your life [your story], he'll do the same thing in you that he did in Jesus, bringing you [your story] alive to himself? When God lives and breathes in you . . . you are delivered from that dead life. With his spirit living in you, your body will be as alive as Christ's! (Rom. 8:10–11, brackets mine)

I want you to do something right now. I want you to pinch yourself.

Go ahead. Did you feel that?

Yup, you are still alive! We're all going to die someday, but that day hasn't come for you yet. Your story here on earth isn't over. Your life has not come to "The End." There is more life for you to live, more that God wants to show you, and more pages still to be written. It doesn't matter where you have been, what you have done, or how ugly the pages looked before today. You are alive. And just like those verses above say, your story can come alive and be made beautiful when God breathes his life into it.

Today you may be walking through a chapter of your life and thinking, *Will this ever end?* I have had times when I wanted the pages to turn faster, wishing that I could read ahead and see what was going to happen in the future. It might be that you are in the early years of your story, just starting out in life. Or maybe you're like me, somewhere in the middle, in the part where it seems like there are lots of transitions and scene changes. Maybe you have kids heading off to college, maybe you are dealing with menopause (fun times!) or even facing retirement. But wherever you are in your story, it is God's desire for it to be filled with pages that reveal his amazing grace and love for you. The twists and turns of our stories don't always go in the direction we'd choose, but if you let God take the pen, he can connect the words of your life to his purpose. Your story can be beautifully interwoven with his!

When you have a little time to spare, take a moment to write out your story. You might think, *Where would I even begin?* You can start anywhere and write whatever is on your heart. Just remember this: God knows your history, and he isn't afraid of it—he can take any story and make it beautiful!

And this is my prayer for you:

*Dear Heavenly Father,*

*As this precious daughter of yours picks up her pen to write, I am asking you to whisper the sweet assurance of your love and care to her heart. May she be aware that nothing about her life has escaped your notice and absolutely nothing about her story causes you to look away. I pray that she would be healed of any shame the enemy wants to trap her in, be set free from any guilt that darkens her heart, and fully understand that you can make every piece of her story beautiful from beginning to end. May she know that you desire to take her past and her present and weave every detail into a future filled with your glorious mercy and grace.*

*Amen.*

## Four

# You Are Loved

We know how much God loves us, and we have put our trust in his love. God is love, and all who live in love live in God, and God lives in them. (1 John 4:16 NLT)

**love:** to delight in, to feel affection for, to like very much

> God loves each of us
> as if there were only one of us.
>
> Augustine

caught his eye, or maybe he caught mine. Either way, I was surprised by the feelings that came when he looked at me or I looked at him. He was tall and noticeable, very noticeable. He was fifteen. I was fifteen. (Mothers, take note. We were way too young!)

The first time we met was in the Sunday school class at church. I don't remember anything about the lesson—not one thing. I just remember meeting the cute guy named John. That afternoon I was invited to the city park to play volleyball with the youth group. He was there, and boy was I so happy.

One year later on a crisp September evening in our quiet little farm town of Fort Morgan, Colorado, we sat in his dad's forest-green Firebird, oblivious to anything else. John and I didn't ever want to stop talking, and we didn't want the night to end. We'd already spent at least an hour on the phone that day after class, but that didn't stop us from coming up with more to say to each other. We talked about anything and everything so we wouldn't have to say good night, while sitting as close to each other as possible, ignoring the impinging console in between us and the worn leather bucket seats.

It was late, and too many minutes past my curfew. Thankfully my parents had grown comfortable with John and were accustomed to our good-night ritual.

"John, I probably need to go inside," I said unconvincingly.

With a smile, he got out of the car, came around and opened my door, took my hand, and started walking with me toward the house. Our steps were slow.

Standing in front of my house, instead of his usual, "Good night, I'll call you tomorrow," he just stood there, holding my hand and looking me in the eyes, then looking at the ground. Repeatedly. It was obvious something serious was on his mind.

"John, what is it?" I was beginning to worry. *Does he have some bad news?*

He hesitated a few seconds more, like he was trying to figure out what to say. Then, clearing his throat, he said in his strong, determined voice, "Debbie . . . I love you."

At that moment, my heart opened up to receive something I'd never had before—John's love. I could not remember ever being happier. He gave me a quick kiss good night, and I watched from the door as he walked back to his car. Actually, I think he may have skipped back to the car (but don't tell him I said that). I went inside, shut the front door, and floated into the kitchen, where my parents were sitting.

My mom looked up from what she was doing, took one look at me, smiled, and said, "John told you he loved you, didn't he?"

I'm not making this up. My parents could see. I'd been given the gift of love, and it showed.

This year John and I celebrated our thirty-third wedding anniversary and 12,045 days of marriage. And I am not ashamed to say I am proud of us. I will admit not every day was bliss, but our marriage is truly amazing and we are committed to keeping it that way. But that's a topic for another book.

Just now, as I was typing this, John walked into the room and said, "I love you!"

I can't tell you how many times he has said those words to me over the years. And the funny thing is, not even once have I held up my hand and said, "John, could you please knock off the 'I love you' stuff? I'm a bit sick of hearing those words from you." No, I don't ever do that. I love being loved. Who doesn't? Deep down, we are all born with the need and desire to know and believe we are loved.

I can only imagine what it would be like never to have heard the words "I love you" or felt the warmth of a hug or the attention of someone who cared for me. But I know there are multitudes of girls out there who have never experienced real, genuine love—those who have been raised in situations that were less than God intended, surrounded by people who didn't provide the affection and love that should have been theirs. Thousands upon thousands of girls experience the heartache of not being loved or the hurt and pain of unloving and broken relationships. It is horribly sad when people cause heartache and pain and do not love like they should. If you, sweet girl, are one of those thousands, I am so sorry.

I am sorry for the hurt and pain that not feeling loved has caused you. I am sorry if you have experienced the devastation of being rejected. I am sorry if you have never been hugged by your mom or dad, or if you are in a marriage in which your husband doesn't show you the affection and love he should. I am sorry if you have never heard the words "I love you" spoken to you, or if those words were only said out of sickening manipulation and not sacrifice.

But whatever hurt you carry from your past, I want you to know this: *you are loved*. I understand that hearing this doesn't take the pain away from what you have experienced in the past. I just want you to know that you are loved and you always have been.

It is my prayer today that the words in this chapter will encourage your heart and give you an understanding of how very much you are loved. I pray too that as you begin to believe those words by faith, you will experience healing from your past and the complete and unconditional love that God, your Heavenly Father, has for you, his daughter. My hope is that through the power of his Word and your heart being open to the truth of what God says about you, your days ahead will be different from your past. That they will be filled with the knowledge that you, precious girl, are adored and cherished. That *you are loved!*

Listen to what John 3:16 says. You may have heard it before, but I can read it over and over again and never get tired of hearing the words.

> For God so greatly loved and dearly prized the world that He [even] gave up His only begotten (unique) Son, so that whoever believes in (trusts in, clings to, relies on) Him shall not perish (come to destruction, be lost), but have eternal (everlasting) life. (AMP-CE)

Do you understand what this means? God loves you a lot, sweet girl. His love for the world includes you! And he demonstrated his love for you in the greatest way possible.

So what exactly does it mean to love? The definition is simple. *To love* means to delight in, feel affection for, and get joy out of caring for someone, and to desire to treasure, cherish, and protect. Isn't that marvelous to think about? Well, it gets even better. Your God and Heavenly Father loves you with that kind of love. He delights in you, feels affection for you, enjoys you, treasures you, cherishes you, and wants to protect and care for you! He created you to be loved by him. And deep within your soul, there is a longing to understand and believe that you are.

God's love is not just a phrase or a concept. God demonstrated his love for you in the greatest way possible. Look back at John 3:16 again, because there are two significant words in the middle of that verse you might have overlooked. They are the words *He gave.* God not only said he loves you but also proved he does by giving you the greatest gift he could possibly give—his Son, Jesus.

My friend, Bible teacher Dick Foth, describes love this way: "Love is the accurate estimate and the adequate supply of someone's need." God loves and cares about everything we need, and the amazing thing is this: he loves us before we ever even acknowledge who he is.

> God shows and clearly proves His [own] love for us by the fact that while we were still sinners, Christ (the Messiah, the Anointed One) died for us. (Rom. 5:8 AMP-CE)

The words in that verse are so incredible to me, because God didn't wait for us to prove ourselves to him. He didn't wait for us to love him first or to clean ourselves up and dress the part so we would be worthy of his love.

He not only demonstrated his love for you by giving you the best gift of all but also gave it even though you were not ready to receive it and didn't deserve it. God loves you so much, and it is his desire that you will come to believe that he does. He is continually trying to reveal his love to you. Even right now!

> With God on your side, how can you lose? If God didn't hesitate to put everything on the line for you, embracing your condition and exposing himself to the worst by sending his own Son, is there anything else he wouldn't gladly and freely do for you? Do you think anyone or anything is going to be able to drive a wedge between you and Christ's love for you? There is no way that is going to happen! Not trouble, not hard times, not hatred of people, not hunger, not homelessness, not threats, not backstabbing, not even the worst sins listed in Scripture.
>
> No matter what happens, nothing can faze you, because Jesus loves you! I am absolutely convinced (and I want you to be too) that nothing—nothing living or dead, angelic or demonic, today or tomorrow, high or low, thinkable or unthinkable—absolutely nothing can get between you and God's love because of the way that Jesus your Master has embraced you. (Rom. 8:31–39, my paraphrase)

No matter where you are at this moment or what you have experienced, you are never outside the reach of God's love. It doesn't matter if you are actively involved in sin. It doesn't matter if you say you don't believe in God. It doesn't matter if you have told God you hate him. It doesn't matter what you see around you that might be causing you to doubt his love.

He hasn't stopped loving you! Ever. And he never will.

You might say, "But, Debbie, you don't know what I've done!"

Over my years in ministry, I have heard girls ask this question over and over again: "How could God love me? I've done this. I've done that. I had an affair. I had sex with my boyfriend. I lie. I am addicted to drugs. I am not lovable!"

Accepting God's love may be difficult because of what you have been taught, because of an experience of seeing human nature at its worst, or because of your own sinfulness. Hurtful experiences or wrongful teaching can taint your view of God's love.

The truth is God loves you. All you need to do is believe it.

*Dear Father God,*

*I ask you in the name of your Son Jesus to make yourself and your love known to the person reading this prayer. She may be walking through a difficult season in life where she just needs to be reminded of how much you love her. Or she may never have heard or been told until now that you love her, and for the very first time she is hearing about your unconditional and perfect love for her.*

*I may not know her name, but you do. I may not understand the hurt and pain she has endured, but you do. I may not have heard her lonely heart crying, but you have. I ask you to reach down from heaven and reveal your altogether amazing love for her. Give her the faith to believe that the love letters in your Word were written for her, and that your love is enough to fill the void and vacancy in her heart and to cover all the hurt and pain of her past.*

*Your Word says you have loved her with an everlasting love. Today, in this moment, I pray that she not only reads those words but also feels your loving arms around her, holding her, caring for her. May your gentle voice whisper into her ear, "I love you, sweet girl . . . and I will love you forever."*

*Amen.*

# BELIEVING . . .

## Changes Your Heart

You're blessed when you get your inside world—
your mind and your heart—put right.
(Matt. 5:8)

# Five

## Faith—It's That Simple

For we live by faith, not by sight. (2 Cor. 5:7 NIV)

**faith:** to believe in something even when it is unseen or doesn't seem possible

Underneath all you think
and all you do lives all you believe.

When I tell you this story, you have to promise not to laugh.

I am deathly afraid of heights. And I mean anything higher than dirt at sea level. I prefer that both of my feet remain on the earth's surface at all times. No mountain climbing for this chick. But several years ago, my stay-on-the-ground-at-all-costs policy was severely tested. John and I, along with our church leadership staff, were at a leadership retreat. We decided to visit Kanakuk Kamps, a national program for kids, to experience their popular Treetops obstacle course together as a "fun" activity (that is definitely a matter of opinion).

When we arrived, the course guide explained that the activity we were all about to experience would require us to be strapped into a full-body harness and clipped to a wire cable "for our safety and protection." Upon hearing that, I broke out in a cold sweat. He went on to tell us that to complete the course, we would have to climb in tandem, harnessed to a partner, ten feet up the trunk of a tree to the first platform and then make our way through thirteen obstacles, each one higher off the ground than the last. These were designed to build your courage and confidence. I personally feel very courageous with my feet firmly on the ground, thank you very much! All of this "fun" would take place with a crowd of people I knew watching from below!

This adventure would be a cinch for John. He had recently traveled to Africa and summited Mount Kilimanjaro. But John knew exactly what I was thinking, so he had started brainwashing me earlier that morning. After years of marriage, he's learned I am stubborn and competitive and that I like to win. So telling me I *can't* do something only makes me want to prove I can. Even if I am afraid. For this challenge, however, John knew it would take some expert coercing on his part to get my feet off the ground. He would have to convince me that I could make it through.

By the time it was our turn to suit up, John had done a good job of convincing me, and I was determined to be brave and conquer my fear and the challenge . . . even though just looking up at it from the ground made me shake. I had to keep reminding myself, *If, as the guide says, a twelve-year-old camper can do this, surely I can.*

Strapping on the harness and getting into the required safety equipment did not ease my concerns. As trainers secured multiple belts and buckles around my body, I thought, *This obviously is not a safe activity. It's very dangerous or we would not have to wear all this stuff!* But I was too proud to back out. I wanted to prove that I could do it, especially to myself.

After checking every buckle and clip multiple times and ensuring everything was set, the trainers tethered John and me together. I listened as they repeated the instructions to us for the third time and tried to keep from hyperventilating. My mind kept wandering to places it shouldn't have. *How many people have died doing this?*

Finally, it was our turn. My legs felt like lead weights as John and the course instructors waited patiently for me to move and take my first step up the ramp to the first platform.

The ramp was made of two large tree logs leaning side by side. I stepped onto the ramp. *That was easy.* Second step. *That wasn't so hard either.* Third step. *Wow, I am actually doing this!* But about halfway up, I made a very bad decision, the worst thing I could have done. I looked down. And to my horror, the ground seemed miles away.

At that moment, not only did I freeze as icy fear swept over me, but to my humiliation and frustration, I also started crying and trembling uncontrollably. You would've thought I was dangling off the torch of the Statue of Liberty or cleaning the windows on the hundredth floor of the Empire State Building without a harness.

Now, remember, we had a deal—you promised you wouldn't laugh!

In my frozen and panicked state, I heard John whisper in my ear, "Debbie, you are only five feet off the ground. I've got you. I won't let go."

*Yeah, right,* I thought. *We'll just both go down together!* I swallowed hard and tried to slow my breathing so I didn't sob out loud.

"Do you believe me?" John said softly.

I nodded. I wanted to believe him and I guess I did, because I kept going. And with a few more short and wobbly steps, we finished the climb up the logs and conquered that first and very dangerous obstacle. We were now a whopping ten feet off the ground!

Ever so slowly, we inched our way through the course. At any moment, I could have said I wanted off and quit, but I didn't. John kept holding my hand and I kept a tight grip on his, choosing to believe that with his help I would make it to the finish. We weren't the fastest pair on the course that day; in fact, we finished last. But we finished! I made it through all thirteen obstacles, and at the top and final platform, fifty feet off the ground, John whispered in my ear, "I told you you could do it; you just had to believe me," and kissed me on the cheek.

John's constant "You can do this" and "You got this" helped me to believe I could make it. I chose to keep listening to him and believing in what I heard him say. If I had not done that, I wouldn't have made it. I would have quit. I can still hear him saying, "Don't look down. Stay focused. You can do this. Keep believing!"

To have faith means to believe in something even if it is unseen or doesn't seem possible. Pretty much everything you believe in takes a level of faith.

Think about it. You believe that:

- the person who cuts your hair knows what they are doing
- the pizza you ordered will be good enough to eat
- the water you drink will be safe and healthy
- going to the dentist is worth the pain
- the chair you're sitting in will hold you up

You are probably just like me in that some actions, like flying on a plane or climbing an obstacle course, take more faith than others. The bottom line is this: we don't like not knowing how things are going to work out, and we are skeptics by nature when we cannot comprehend something with our own human understanding. We like to see and understand things before we believe in them.

There is a chapter in the Bible known as the faith chapter, and it describes faith this way:

Now faith is the assurance . . . of the things [we] hope for, being the proof of things [we] do not see and the conviction of their reality. (Heb. 11:1 AMP-CE)

It's very simple, really. Faith is what gives you the confidence to believe in things that you cannot yet see or understand through your human eyes.

My daughter, Savannah, has always held very strong convictions. Even as a little girl, when she believed in something, she committed to it. When our three children were in elementary school, John and I made the decision to homeschool them for a variety of reasons. The most important reason was to give John more time with them during the day, as our weekend and night schedules were often filled with the needs of pastoring a very active and growing church.

On the first day of school, I was very excited as I reviewed the lessons I had prepared the week before: math, English, reading, and science. When I got dressed that morning, I had selected my most teacher-ish outfit, with an apple necklace someone had given me to complete the look (those were memorable days in the fashion world). I proudly checked my supplies neatly arranged on the little oak kitchen table in the tiny apartment we were renting at the time: textbooks, pencils, paper. Check, check, check.

Earth science was the first subject of the day. We didn't have an actual globe, so I had a large navel orange ready to represent the earth. I had used a Sharpie to draw the world's continents on the shiny peel. Hopefully the kids wouldn't notice Australia was missing, since I ran out of room on my orange prop. My apologies to all my Aussie friends.

With my three sweet children all in place at the table, I confidently instructed them to open their science books to chapter 1. "Today our very first lesson is about the earth and its shape," I said with a smile. I proudly picked up my little orange globe. "This is what the earth looks like from space. It's round like an orange."

That was as far as I got. My first sentence of teaching was interrupted with a shout of disagreement.

"No, it's not, Mom," Savannah blurted out. "You're wrong."

*What is she talking about?*

"The earth is flat," she continued.

I wasn't quite ready for this. I started over in my calm, trying-to-sound-like-a-teacher voice. "Actually, no, it's not, Savannah. The earth is round like a ball. See?" I held up my fruity example again. I had loved object lessons when I was in school, and I just knew my kids would too. How could they not be convinced?

"No, it's not," Savannah said again, with enough strength and emotion to almost convince me I was wrong.

"Yes, it is," I said in the determined voice of a science professor.

With that, Savannah burst out crying, jumped off her chair, and ran across the living room and out onto the third-story balcony. With her finger pointing across the back parking lot, she sobbed, "No, it's not. Look, it's flat. It's flat!"

To know Savannah is to know a person with strong convictions and commitment to her beliefs. Once she was convinced the earth was flat, not even her mother, wearing a jean jumper and holding a very round orange, could change her belief.

Somehow we finally called a truce that day. I decided it really didn't matter at this moment in her life if my daughter believed the world was flat. Eventually she came around, and thankfully today she is in full agreement with Galileo.

Like Savannah, you can start to believe things that are not actually true. If you are not careful, you can put your confidence in your own thinking and in only what you can see, rather than in what God's Word says.

Ultimately, walking by faith and believing what God says is a choice. Each and every day we all come face-to-face with situations and obstacles in life that will invoke a response, and inevitably our human nature will respond first out of fear based on what we see and humanly understand. It is natural. That is why 2 Corinthians 5:7 says, "We live by faith, not by sight" (or what we see). The New Living Translation says, "We live by believing and not by seeing."

To believe in God and what he says in his Word is a decision you have to make—it is your heart responding by faith.

Look at these amazing words in 1 Peter 1:8–9:

> You never saw him [Jesus], yet you love him. You still don't see him, yet you trust him—with laughter and singing. Because you kept on believing, you'll get what you're looking forward to: total salvation. (brackets mine)

We tend to make faith in God too complicated. Really, it is very simple. It's making a choice to trust and believe that what he says is true. That's all. And when you do, a miracle happens. An assurance and a confidence begin to fill your heart and soul that override what you don't know and can't control. It doesn't mean that you immediately see everything clearly, nor is every question about life answered. But the truth is your faith connected to your Creator has immense power. It enables you to look at your life from an "I trust and believe God" point of view.

What do you believe? What are you putting your faith in today?

When you start putting your faith in God, he promises to help you. As followers of Jesus, we are all working to grow in faith. And his greatest desire is that we would trust him in everything—even the things we can't see or understand.

Remember that verse in Hebrews 11:1 that we talked about earlier? *The Message* puts it this way:

> This faith . . . is the firm foundation under everything that makes life worth living. It's our handle on what we can't see.

One of the hardest things for me as a leader in the church is watching girls who sit stagnant in their faith. They have made the decision to believe in God for their salvation, but that is as far as they go. They don't seem to move forward but stay stuck at the bottom level or are barely inching along. They have very weak faith. Consequently they live weak and unproductive lives, missing out on the joy of believing that God has more for them than just surviving. They don't do the things they need to do to keep growing and moving forward. And they miss out on experiencing the thrilling adventure of the treetops and the view that comes from growing in faith.

Here's the deal: your faith in God and in what he says about you, your life, and your future should be stronger today than it was when you first believed in him. Your faith should be growing—it is not at any point meant to stay at the same level.

Listen to what Paul writes to the believers in Colossians:

> Let your roots grow down into him, and let your lives be built on him. Then your faith will grow strong in the truth you were taught, and you will overflow with thankfulness. (2:7 NLT)

Your faith is meant to be alive, active, and flourishing, like a healthy tree with deep roots in the soil of the knowledge of who God is. And just like that verse says, my desire is that you would continue to grow stronger and stronger in your faith and live a vibrant, believing life!

A life overflowing with faith and confidence in God.

A life that displays faith through your words and actions.

A life that withstands the trials and tests that come your way.

A life that reveals faith to everyone around you!

---

I want to leave you with a few steps to help you grow in faith:

Ask God to help you to grow in your faith.

Take time each day to read your Bible. The book of Mark is a great place to start.

Memorize verses in the Bible that talk about faith. Start with Hebrews 11:1.

Find a Bible-believing church and get involved in it. If you don't
know where to go, I invite you to visit http://jamesriver.org.

Hang around girls who are growing in their faith.

Remember, we are all in this together!

I would love to share more with you about faith and trust in
God. Visit me online at www.debbielindell.com.

# Six

# Prayer—a Difference Maker

And whatever you ask for in prayer, having faith and [really] believing, you will receive. (Matt. 21:22 AMP-CE)

**prayer:** open, honest, and expectant conversation with God

I pray because I can't help myself. I pray
because I'm helpless. I pray because the need flows
out of me all the time—waking and sleeping.
It doesn't change God—it changes me.

C. S. Lewis

One of the most wonderful things about walking with God is that you get to have a personal and real relationship with him. God isn't just a surreal figure somewhere hanging out in space. He is in every way real and wanting to be actively involved in the lives of humanity, especially those who are seeking to know him. And his desire is to have a personal and interactive relationship with you, strengthening you and daily helping you to navigate the situations that are a part of living your life here on earth.

How, you might ask? Through prayer. God wants you to talk to him, to tell him about your hopes, your dreams, and the things you need his help with.

When you think about what it means to pray, it may very well conjure up different ideas or memories. Perhaps one of them is from your childhood, when you knelt beside your bed at night repeating words you didn't fully understand, such as, "Now I lay me down to sleep, I pray the Lord my soul to keep. . . ." Maybe you picture your family holding hands around the table, while your mom or dad prayed a blessing over the food. Or you might remember a preacher reciting a prayer from a pulpit in the church that you went to as a child. Maybe you have never really known what it means to pray, and the whole idea is uncomfortable to you. I can understand that.

I made the decision to follow God when I was a very young girl, but to be honest, I am still learning how to talk to him and share my thoughts and needs with him every day. My opinion is that learning to pray is a lifetime process, and wherever you are in that journey, it is my hope that you will continue to grow in your understanding of what it means to have your very own personal prayer relationship with God.

I look at prayer as a relationship with a very good friend. We might talk to a friend about things we are experiencing in life, our feelings about something, or the struggles we are facing. It is the same with our relationship with God, only a hundred times better.

God is the ultimate best friend. We can talk to him about absolutely everything and ask for his help with absolutely anything. And he is always ready to listen and give us his undivided attention. He is never too busy or distracted by other things around him. He's the best listener ever!

Though I am still growing in my faith, in my relationship with God, and in learning how to pray, over the years I have come to understand more and more that God loves to hear me talk to him—anytime and all the time. He is downright jealous for me to run to him first and talk to him about the situations and challenges that I face in life. He wants me to trust and believe that he is always ready to help with anything I am going through.

One night, years ago, I needed God's help in a very big way.

John and I had been walking through a very difficult season. We were under tremendous stress and pressure in our ministry and marriage, and it was affecting our home in a big way. On that particular night in the fall of 2001, I was at a breaking point.

I can remember that night so clearly. With tired feet and a very discouraged heart, I slowly made my way from the garage up the wood steps into the house. I glanced at the door frame and thought about the entrance into our home—the one John and I walk through each day as we leave for work and then come back through at night. The days were especially long right now.

John was at a board meeting at church, the kids were gone, and other than our dog, Tramp, greeting me with his long, furry, wagging tail, the house was quiet. I stopped on the last step, staring at the door, thinking about how John would be coming through that same door later tonight, and wondering, *What can I do to stop what is happening to us?*

For months now, nothing had been normal. We'd been walking through a very difficult and pressure-packed year, including challenges I never dreamed we would face. I had sensed John becoming increasingly detached from me, and I was worried, knowing he was under more pressure than ever with a fast-growing church to pastor, a large building project to oversee, and the unexpected loss of his best friend to deal with. Not to mention trying to be a husband to me (his discouraged wife) and a father to three very active teenagers.

As I stood staring at the door, my emotions boiled over and tears welled up in my eyes. The days at work were becoming harder, our nights were filled with too much quiet, and my mind was fighting against the pull to spin out of control with doubts and faithless thoughts.

*What if there's a hidden reason he seems detached? What if there's more to all of this than the stress of the circumstances? Could he be having an affair? What if our marriage and our ministry are actually falling apart?*

As I stood there, I voiced a simple prayer with as much strength as I could manage. "God, I need your help."

I had been praying and talking to God about this for weeks, but tonight was different. Tonight I was desperate for him to help me. And right there in the stillness of our garage, right next to our lawn mower, I heard God whisper this gentle but firm question: *Debbie, do you really believe I can help you?*

I knew the answer. But it was obvious that the days of struggle and stress had begun to wear down my belief and trust. And I realized then and there that I needed to put some jumper cables on my faith!

I quickly assessed my position and what I believed deep in my heart to be true. God was with me, and he cared about what John and I were going through. And if I looked to him in faith, believing, he wanted to help me.

With that, I walked into the house with renewed determination. I was tired of this battle and I was going to fight back—in prayer. I set my purse and grocery bags down on the little bench in the mudroom and marched down the hall toward the kitchen.

*I'm going to stand on the truth of what God in his Word says about me, and I'm going to pray like I've never prayed before. I am going to fight this attack on my marriage, my home, my family, and our ministry with everything I have! I am not going to let Satan win. Because I know what God's Word says: "She will call on me, and I will answer her; I will be with her in trouble, I will deliver her."* (see Ps. 91:15 NIV).

And then, right there in our kitchen, I started praying out loud.

"God, I am in desperate need of help. John and I are walking through a huge trial. We are in a battle! Our marriage is definitely not what it should be, and our home is becoming more and more silent and lifeless. I don't understand what is happening, and on my own I don't know what to do. *But* what I do know is this. I believe with all my heart that it is not your will for my marriage to fail. It is not your will for our ministry to fall apart. It is your will for them to flourish and be strong and vibrant. So tonight I stand on the truth of who you say you are. I am asking for your help, and I believe that *you are* going to help me! Amen."

I didn't stop with that one prayer. No, I was fighting to win.

I put on my spiritual marching boots, and for the next several hours, with steely determination, I marched through our house praying in every room—the kitchen, the family room, the office, our bedroom, the bathroom, and the closet. And as I prayed, I sensed God speaking to my heart not only to pray for the battle in our marriage but to pray specifically for my husband and the battle he was in. So I did. I prayed over John's coffee mug, the desk in his office, his chair, his side of the mirror in our bathroom, all of his shoes in our closet, and our bed. I prayed specifically, like I believed God was right there asking me what I needed him to do. And each time I opened my mouth, my voice became stronger. I had no doubt that my Heavenly Father was listening to me, his daughter.

And the most amazing thing began to happen! The longer I prayed, the more I could sense the confusion, doubt, and despair being stripped away from my soul. My faith was building with each statement of belief, filling my heart with a renewed confidence, hope, and anticipation that an answer was on the way.

I love what the psalmist writes about prayer:

> In my distress I called to the Lord;
>   I cried to my God for help.
> From his temple he heard my voice;
>   my cry came before him, into his ears. (Ps. 18:6 NIV)

And then the writer tells us that God says this:

> Call on Me in the day of trouble; I will deliver you, and you shall honor and glorify Me. (Ps. 50:15 AMP-CE)

What a comforting thought. God is listening for my voice. God is big enough to handle my need. And God cares enough to respond and help me when I ask him to.

And that is exactly what was about to happen.

Late that night, when John finally walked up those same steps in our garage, he had no idea that he was entering into a different home than the one he had left hours before. I knew I was different too.

It was after midnight now, and I was in bed still praying when John silently crawled under the covers next to me. It was obvious that the thousand-pound weight of stress he had been carrying for weeks now was still there. And even though I didn't know what was going to happen next, I was now sure that God was going to help us no matter what we were facing.

With my heart beating full speed inside my chest, I whispered, "John." And then, taking a deep breath, I summoned the courage to ask him the question nagging at my soul—the one that had been sitting in the back corner of my mind for nearly a month now. "Are you having an affair?"

John's response was quick and sure. "Debbie, are you kidding me? I can't handle my life as it is. When would I ever have time for another woman?!"

If his answer hadn't been so heart-wrenching, I might have laughed. He was right. He was working night and day, coming home exhausted from this season of seemingly endless meetings and ministry. Most nights he fell asleep on the couch within minutes of walking through the door, too tired to add one more conversation to his day.

But God used that moment and my question to begin answering my cries for help. It was as if a ray of light entered our bedroom and a rope was dropped down from heaven for us to grab on to, pulling us to safety. There in the wee hours of the morning, after weeks of little or no communication, John began to open up and talk about how emotionally and physically exhausted he was. He willingly acknowledged that things needed to change. I joined in, opening up about my feelings of discouragement and my fears about our marriage. I told him how for several hours that night, I had prayed for God to do a miracle in our home and in both of our hearts. And for the first time in weeks, we held each other and prayed together about the stress-filled season of life we were facing. And right then and there, the miracle I had asked for began to take place.

Now, just so you know, our life and marriage didn't suddenly snap into perfection. But everything about our situation and the way we were looking at things began to change. I had no doubt that God was at work, he had heard my cry for his help, and he was answering my prayer.

Today John and I both look back at that season in our marriage and ministry as a time when Satan was doing everything he could to destroy God's plan. If we had not looked to God by faith to help us, the outcome could have been very different.

During the weeks leading up to that night, I had gradually let the circumstances we were walking through whittle away at my trust and confidence in God. The fact is, I still have moments when the stresses and pressures of life want to take hold of my thoughts. I have days when doubt can weigh me down, and there are nights when my mind wants to spin out of control. Just like anyone else, I have to fight to trust that God is going to take care of the situation I am facing.

Here's the deal: we have to choose not to worry and to believe that God is bigger than our problems. The Word of God is very clear that worry and believing God don't mix.

Look at these words in Philippians 4:6–7:

Do not be anxious about anything, but in every situation, by prayer and petition, with thanksgiving, present your requests to God. And the peace of God, which transcends all understanding, will guard your hearts and your minds in Christ Jesus. (NIV)

Did you catch that? Do not be anxious or worried about anything. Not one thing! And give everything to God. *Everything!* The big things and the little things.

How, you might ask? By praying and asking for his help, and then, being thankful in advance, believing that he is going to help you. As you do that, a supernatural calmness will settle like a soft blanket on your heart and mind, completely changing your thinking and replacing your worry with faith. Amazing!

Believing in God is one thing. Believing God is everything you need, and that he is there in every situation to listen when you pray and take your worry away, is a whole different level of belief.

Let me ask you this question. What are you facing today that seems too big for you to handle? What are you up against that is causing you to lay awake at night, conjuring up fearful thoughts about your future?

Are you in need of a job? God can help you.

Did you get an unexpected bill in the mail? God can provide.

Is your child out of control? God can give you strength and wisdom as a parent.

Is your marriage in trouble? God can heal your broken home.

Are you confused and overwhelmed by a decision you need to make? God can show you what to do.

I believe that God is speaking to your heart right now and wants your faith to go to another level. And it will, as you start responding to situations with a different perspective—a faith-filled one.

Now, I want you to hear this. If you have never really prayed before, or you are just learning how to pray, it can be intimidating. Why is that? Because Satan wants to do everything he can to keep you from praying. And a part of his strategy is to make you feel insecure and even afraid to pray—to make you think that you aren't good enough, that you have to pray in a certain way, at a certain time, and use the perfect words in order for God to listen. None of that is true. Those are just lies and distractions to keep you from openly and freely talking to God.

I love the simplicity in which Dietrich Bonhoeffer, a German pastor and theologian in the mid-1900s, explained prayer. "We are privileged to know that he knows our needs before we ask him. This is what gives Christian prayer its boundless confidence and its joyous certainty. It matters little what form of prayer we adopt or how many words we use, what matters is the faith which lays hold on God and touches the heart of the Father who knew us long before we came to him."[1]

When you pray, the only thing that is important to God is whether you believe him—that he cares enough to listen, respond, and help you. Because he does!

Look at these beautiful words about prayer in James 1:

> If you don't know what you're doing, pray to the Father. He loves to help. You'll get his help, and won't be condescended to when you ask for it. Ask boldly, believingly, without a second thought. (vv. 5–7)

God wants to help you, my friend. Do you believe that? He really does. He won't be thinking, *What is wrong with her—why didn't she come to me before now about this?* He will just be happy that you finally decided to stop worrying and believe that he is there, bending down to listen and help you with whatever it is you need.

Before you turn the page, I want to encourage you to stop right now, wherever you are, and pray. If you are in a setting where you don't feel you can pray very loud, that's okay—he can hear a whisper too. Don't worry if your words don't sound perfect. He doesn't care about that. He will just be so excited that you are talking to him and asking for his help. I promise this—as you pray, your faith will begin to grow, courage and confidence will rise up in your heart, and peace will flood your soul. And most importantly, God, your Heavenly Father, will stop and listen, and he will help you!

That, my friend, is a fact. And here is my prayer for you:

*Dear Heavenly Father,*

*I am asking you to speak to the heart of my friend. I pray that you would help her to gain a fresh understanding of what it means to have a close relationship with you, just like that of a best friend. One where she feels confident to talk to you about anything and believes that you are listening and responding when she does.*

*Amen.*

## *Seven*

# Following Is Leading

Pattern yourself after me [follow my example], as I imitate and follow Christ. (1 Cor. 11:1 AMP-CE)

---

**lead•ing:** showing the way to those who are following; initiating movement

When you are following Jesus,
no matter where you go,
you will never be lost.

Have you ever heard a parent say to their child, "Stop being a leader. You need to be a follower"? Probably not. But it is very possible that you've heard these words from a parent, teacher, or coach: "Come on, now, be a leader!"

Being a leader is what we are taught to aspire to. And isn't being a leader what we all really want to do? When you're the leader, you get to:

- choose your own direction
- proceed at your own pace
- chart your own course
- make your own way
- listen to yourself

There seems to be something inside most of us that loves to do what *we* want to do. Remember playing Simon Says as a kid? If you got to be Simon, you yelled out the directives. You were the one in charge, and it made you feel important. On the other hand, bending to the will of someone else can be one of the hardest things you will ever do. The act of following requires everything human nature fights against:

- submission
- humility
- concentration
- a commitment to someone else's direction
- the selfless decision to stop going your own way

To follow well means you have to give the leader your full attention, listen, and imitate what they do. Following requires the total yielding of one's will to the will of another. Jesus told us it would require just that to follow him, plus leaving everything else behind. He didn't say it would be easy. In fact, he said it would be difficult, requiring you to deny your own desires, lose yourself, and crucify your will. I don't know about you, but that doesn't exactly sound inviting to me. Even though it goes directly against everything inside our human nature, the truth is, following Jesus closely is the key to your spirit coming alive to all that is good and right and true. This is how Jesus explained it:

> Anyone who intends to come with me has to let me lead. You're not in the driver's seat—I am. (Luke 9:23)

What people don't understand is that when you give up your will and desire to direct your own life in order to submit to and follow Jesus, he will lead you to find everything you have been searching for. Every desire, longing, hope, and dream is found in following him. I love how the psalmist words it:

> You will show me [lead me to] the path of life; in Your presence is fullness of joy, at Your right hand there are pleasures forevermore. (Ps. 16:11 AMP-CE, brackets mine)

Following after God through his Son Jesus—staying close to him, being guided by him, and enjoying his presence every moment of every day—is what leads you to a fully satisfying and fulfilled life.

As we continue to spend time together through the words in this book, more than anything it is my desire that you will be inspired and challenged to live close to Jesus. That your life will be changed as you draw closer to him and are encouraged to grow stronger in your faith. I want you to hear Jesus saying to you, "Come follow me, believe in me, and I will show you the path of life!"

While he was on earth, Jesus was constantly inviting people to follow him. The problem was people didn't always like what it would mean for them. They liked the idea of being with Jesus and associating with him, but when they understood what it would cost to be his true follower, that was often the end of their commitment.

In Luke chapter 14, Jesus was traveling and teaching, and crowds were around him everywhere he went. They were taken with the miracles they saw him do and probably enjoyed the free food as well (lots of fish and bread). Jesus was cool and the talk of the town. It was hip to follow him around. But Jesus could see inside their hearts, and he knew some of those following him liked what they saw only as long as they didn't have to sacrifice anything or give up their way of life. They loved his gifts, not the life he was calling them to. So he took time to explain clearly what it meant to be his true follower.

> Anyone who comes to me but refuses to let go of father, mother, spouse, children, brothers, sisters—yes, even one's own self!— can't be my disciple. Anyone who won't shoulder his own cross and follow behind me can't be my disciple. . . . Simply put, if you're not willing to take what is dearest to you, whether plans or people, and kiss it good-bye, you can't be my disciple. (vv. 26–27, 33)

Whew! Those are strong words. When a person chooses to follow Jesus, it is not without cost. You have to be willing to go where he leads you and, if necessary, give up the so-called comfort of living your own way. Sometimes it is even at the cost of losing a relationship with someone in your own family, if they do not choose to follow him with you.

Some people decide it's just too costly to follow Jesus. You may know someone like that. They decide that the price is just too high. It can mean losing your job and income, being made fun of and ridiculed, having to let go of a friendship, or leaving behind the pleasure of sin you are enjoying.

Several years ago, John and I went to visit a single mom named Carla who had visited our church. When she cautiously answered the door of her small apartment, it was obvious she was not doing well. She was pale and thin and looked like she had been crying.

"Are you okay?" I asked.

"Yes," Carla said unconvincingly. "I was just reading a sappy part of a romance novel before you knocked at the door, and it was making me cry."

John and I looked at each other, a little suspicious of her explanation. She wouldn't let us in but seemed willing to talk. We introduced ourselves, told her why we were there, and asked her what had brought her to our church and if she had any questions. She told us she had not been in church for years, and this was the first time she had visited James River Church.

John had preached that Sunday on what the Bible says about giving to God. She brought up the message and how it had encouraged her, then told us she couldn't stop crying when she got into her car after the service. With that, she began to cry again. As we stood there, this precious girl opened up and shared her story with us. She was a single mom working as a stripper, and she and her children were living with a man who was abusing her. Then she said how afraid she was. She was afraid of her boyfriend, afraid of quitting her job, afraid of losing her income, and afraid of leaving him because she wouldn't have any money or anywhere to live.

The message on giving had moved her heart. She just had to decide if she could give up the security of what little she had to trust and follow Jesus. Right before we showed up at her door, Carla had been crying out to God and asking him to help her, saying, "I will trust and follow you, but I need you to help me and show me what to do." And then, out of nowhere, she heard us knocking on her door!

We prayed with Carla right there. We told her we would do everything we could to help her, but she would need to make some changes in her life. She agreed. As John and I turned to leave, wondering what to do, we knew if we prayed and believed, God would show us an answer for this girl. I had no sooner climbed into the truck and shut the door when I heard the name of a family whispered to my heart. "John, I think we need to call the Tylers and see if they might temporarily take in Carla and her two kids." I called from my cell phone, and Susan Tyler answered. Within twenty minutes, Carla and her family had a brand-new place to call home, and her brand-new life of following Jesus had begun.

Carla made the decision by faith to leave her life behind and go in a completely different direction—where Jesus was leading her. With that decision, everything about her life completely changed for the better. Everything. Today she is married and her kids are following Jesus too.

Following Jesus with all your heart doesn't mean everything is going to go smoothly and you will never have any challenges. But it does mean you will have a satisfied and abundantly blessed journey through life, and as you let him lead, you can be sure he will take you on the best and most beautiful route.

I love the following verses. You have probably heard them before and maybe even know them by heart.

The Lord is my Shepherd [to feed, guide, and shield me], I shall not lack.

He makes me lie down in [fresh, tender] green pastures; He leads me beside the still and restful waters.

He refreshes and restores my life (my self); He leads me in the paths of righteousness [uprightness and right standing with Him—not for my earning it, but] for His name's sake.

Yes, though I walk through the [deep, sunless] valley of the shadow of death, I will fear or dread no evil, for You are with me; Your rod [to protect] and Your staff [to guide], they comfort me. . . .

Surely or only goodness, mercy, and unfailing love shall follow me all the days of my life, and through the length of my days the house of the Lord [and His presence] shall be my dwelling place. (Ps. 23:1–4, 6 AMP-CE)

What a beautiful description that is of what we will experience when we follow closely to Jesus. No matter what we go through, he will be right there to watch over us, to bless us, and to lead us home.

We all do better when we're not leading ourselves. If the path seems a bit dark or is a little blurry, and if you can't see where it's leading, just keep your eyes fixed on Jesus. I promise he will lead you well and you will never be lost. I don't always know where I'm going and can't always see where I'm heading, but with Jesus leading me, I can know I'm on a path that will lead me to the right places!

One last thought. Always remember that following is leading! Who you follow determines where you lead those watching you. If you are following people who are not honoring and obeying God, then you yourself will begin imitating them and leading those watching and following you to do the same.

But if you are following Jesus and seeking to honor him in all you do, with confidence you can invite everyone to watch and follow you.

Paul understood that when he said these words:

Pattern yourselves after me [follow my example], as I imitate and follow Christ. (1 Cor. 11:1 AMP-CE)

He could confidently encourage others to watch him, imitate him, and follow him, because he was following Jesus so closely.

One of the most exciting and incredible aspects of following Jesus closely is that you can, with confidence, invite others to follow you. I don't know about you, but that excites me. Honestly, my greatest desire in life is to be someone whom others can follow. Having that desire gives me a greater resolve and determination to keep my eyes on Jesus—not to look behind or beside or ahead of him but to commit to fixing my eyes on him and staying as close to him as possible so nothing clouds my view.

So with that, my friend, let me encourage you. Look to Jesus, following him as closely as you can, and then you can be sure that you will lead others to follow him too.

## *Eight*

# It's Foolish Not to Be Wise

Don't miss a word of this—I'm telling you how
to live well,
I'm telling you how to live at your best.

Proverbs 8:6

**wis•dom:** knowing and doing what is best, true, and right; good judgment, discernment, insight

It is never too late to become
the person you want to be.

When John and I were in our third year of marriage, we made a decision not to watch television in our home. We had several reasons, but most importantly, we mutually agreed that it would be best for our kiddos, our marriage, our home life, and our desire to grow in God. It wasn't that we thought watching television was sinful; it was just not beneficial during that season of our lives.

Our sons, David and Brandon, were toddlers, and Savannah was just a baby. I was in that mommy season of life, home alone most of the time doing mommy things, like changing lots of poopy diapers, wiping runny noses, making animal sounds with the kids, picking up toys, and answering the question "Why, Mommy?" a hundred times a day. Although I loved being a mom, with three little ones requiring my constant attention, I had moments when I felt isolated from the entire world, and I struggled with feeling that life was passing me by.

Even though we had made the decision not to watch TV, we still owned one. Our media center consisted of a thirteen-inch box tucked away in the unfinished basement of our house, on a shelf near our washer and dryer underneath the stairs. One particular winter day, I was struggling with those "all I do is change diapers" mommy feelings more than usual. But instead of replacing those thoughts with something good and worthwhile, I let my mind wander to a place it shouldn't have.

So while the boys were napping, I opened the basement door and made my way down the unfinished stairway with three-month-old Savannah in tow. I laid her down on the old, worn-out sofa someone had donated to us, headed toward the washer and dryer, pulled out the little TV, and proceeded to set it up on the concrete floor.

All the while a voice was screaming in my head, *Debbie, stop, don't do this. Debbie, you made a promise. Debbie, this is not wise!* But I didn't listen. I didn't want to listen. Instead, I turned on the TV. And just to be safe, in case John came home unexpectedly, I carefully and strategically positioned it in front of the narrow little basement window that faced our driveway. How perfect! The placement would buy me time to hide the evidence if I needed to. Nice plan.

Still, there was that voice again. *Debbie, what in the world are you doing? STOP!*

But I didn't want to stop, and I began to flip through the channels to scope out what was on TV during nap time that would make my life more interesting. Not much. But then something caught my attention and I paused, intrigued by what I saw. It was a daytime show I'd heard girls talk about before, and it looked and sounded exciting and romantic. I didn't watch much that day. That voice in my head kept interrupting me, and I felt guilty the whole ten minutes the TV was on. But what I didn't know is that those ten minutes were like chocolate to my brain, and the next day I would want some more.

The program I'd stumbled on was *General Hospital*. And its story line was filled with sex, affairs, lying, and scandalous be-havior. Within a week, I was hooked and started planning my afternoon schedule so I could have the little TV out and in position before the program started. The two main characters, Luke and

Laura, were embroiled in an epic and sinful love affair. Not only was I mesmerized by the story, but I was also becoming addicted to it.

And that voice, the one that kept telling me I was being foolish? Well, I was successfully shoving it to the back of my brain.

Each day of my new routine, I experienced a mixture of both excitement and frustration. I knew what I was doing was wrong, partly because John and I had made a commitment and I wasn't being honest and living up to it, and partly because I knew that for me, watching the show was sinful, as it was filled with things that were not honoring to God. The show's content and my actions were causing me to think on things that were not beneficial to anything in my life, such as my marriage, my kids, being a mom, or my relationship with God. I was not gaining anything. I was actually losing my peace of mind, my integrity, and my truthfulness; compromising my desire to honor God; and sacrificing what I really wanted to be—a wise mom, wife, friend, and leader. And for what? A TV show.

It wasn't that I didn't know what to do. God was constantly trying to get my attention with his loving voice of wisdom. The bottom line was I was choosing foolishness. I was totally aware that what I was doing was wrong, and in a very short amount of time, my sinful and unwise choices began to build a wall of guilt and condemnation around my heart, causing a separation from my dearest friend in the world, Jesus.

Looking back, I regret what I did because it was just plain sad and ridiculous! If for some reason the boys didn't nap during that time of day, I would make them sit down on the cement with me and play quietly. And if I saw John pull in the driveway, I'd panic, rush to get the TV hidden, and then act like I was doing laundry in the basement.

Sin and foolishness are such a trap. They have a way of confusing us and blurring our spiritual vision. And the longer we cater to them, the thicker the wall of confusion gets and the greater the distance in our minds between right and wrong.

Finally, one day my frustration with my sinful, foolish self came to a boiling point in my soul. My desire to have my relationship with Jesus restored to wholeness, for my heart to be free from guilt, and for my mind to be free from the lure of this sin became greater than my desire for the pleasure from it. So I made the decision to stop what I was doing.

Was it easy? No, not especially. I had to make the wise choice and then discipline myself to keep making it. I had to leave behind what I was enjoying for what I knew was best. I had to choose to quit catering to my foolish desire and respond to the voice of wisdom and rightness in my soul. With determination and by God's grace, I did it, and I am so thankful for that. I replaced what was worthless and destructive to my soul with things that were valuable, life giving, and wise, not only for me personally but also for my marriage, my family, and my desire to be an example of wisdom to those around me.

And even though I missed them at first, Luke and Laura never missed me, not even once! That experience taught me so much. Most importantly, I learned that being wise was a choice, and I could choose to be a wise girl or a foolish one.

Making the choice to walk through life in wisdom has nothing to do with having a high IQ and little, if anything, to do with a degree you have achieved or where you graduated from. You, like me, have probably met some very intelligent and knowledgeable people. When you listen to those people talk, you are made aware of things you do not know and may never understand. The truth is there are a lot of people who are smarter than me in a whole lot of things, but that doesn't exclude me from being able to walk in wisdom and make wise decisions.

I don't know about you, but that is so comforting to me.

Now, don't get me wrong—I am all about learning. Knowledge is valuable and necessary for being all that God wants us to be. And experience can make your life easier, as in "Oops! I don't think I'll do *that* again."

Several years ago, I was in a large and busy bathroom at a huge convention center. When I went to wash my hands, I noticed that the counters were all wet and slimy because of the soap drippings. So I decided to put my oversized and very cool travel purse (filled with every necessity a girl needs for a convention) in one of the sinks to keep it from getting slimy. I set it down in the driest sink I could find, then moved to wash my hands in the next sink. After I'd finished washing and drying my hands and looked in the mirror to see if my lip color needed touching up, I turned to grab my makeup bag out of my purse. Now, if you are smarter than me, you probably guessed what happened. My purse was now filled and overflowing with water, and most of the contents were floating on top! I learned something new and very valuable that day. Do not put cute purses in sinks with automatic faucets.

What was I thinking? Obviously I wasn't!

Learning is a good thing! You can see from my purse story that knowledge is valuable for many reasons, including everyday life situations. But having a level of knowledge or book learning is not a prerequisite for you to be a wise person. You can be a very wise girl if you choose to be.

One of my favorite verses in the Bible is found in the book of James:

If any of you lacks wisdom, you should ask God, who gives generously to all without finding fault, and it will be given to you. (1:5 NIV)

God wants to give us wisdom for everything in life. He wants to help us do life well, make good decisions, and be wise friends, sisters, daughters, wives, mothers, and grandmas. In every part of life—in your schooling, in your dating relationships, at work, in your home, in your friendships, in your marriage, with your finances, and in every decision—he wants you to have his wisdom to handle everything wisely.

I love everything about that verse, especially the first four words: "If any of you." How amazing is that! No prequalification needed. No one is exempt. You—yes, you—are welcome to go to God and ask him to give you wisdom.

Look at that verse again, because there is even more good news. Not only does God give his wisdom to *anyone* who asks, but he also gives *without finding fault*. He doesn't look down on us for the reasons we're asking for wisdom. You may have made a poor decision, and you may even feel like you've made a mess of your life because of that decision. You might even be thinking that the mess you've made is too big or too bad for God to fix. But it's not.

It doesn't matter what foolish decisions you have made in the past; God wants to give you wisdom to help you turn things around! He doesn't look at you and wonder, *Why did she do that? Why is she so stupid? Why didn't she just listen to me in the first place?* He just wants to help you!

During my years in ministry, I have watched girl after girl make foolish choices because they were popular or easier or seemed like the only solution. Quite honestly, it breaks my heart when I see girls make choices and decisions that bring hurt and pain into their lives. But it is even sadder to me when they feel like they have no way out. God does not disqualify us from receiving his help because of what we have done. He is always, always there to give us guidance and wisdom if we ask him to help us out of our messes.

The book of Proverbs was written by King Solomon, who God said was the wisest man who ever lived. He talks about the incredible difference wisdom makes in the life of a person:

> So, my dear friends, listen carefully;
> those who embrace these my ways [of wisdom]
> are most blessed.

> Mark a life of discipline and live wisely;
>> don't squander your precious life.
> Blessed the man, blessed the woman, who listens to me,
>> awake and ready for me each morning,
>> alert and responsive. . . .
> When you find me, you find life, real life,
>> to say nothing of God's good pleasure.
> But if you wrong [ignore] me, you damage your very soul;
>> when you reject me, you're flirting with death.
>> (Prov. 8:32–36, brackets mine)

Maybe you should read that again! The point is very clear and very powerful. Foolishness destroys your life, damages your soul, and leads to death. Not a pretty thought! Proverbs 19:3 reiterates this when it says,

> People ruin their lives by their own stupidity.

But here is the good news. Just as the way of foolishness and sinfulness leads to death, the opposite is true with walking in wisdom. The way of wisdom leads to *life*! The Bible says it leads to real life—a flourishing life filled with God's goodness, blessing, and favor. Here is a little equation to help you remember:

Foolish decisions = Death
Wise decisions = Life

Sounds like an easy choice to make. So why don't more people choose wisdom over foolishness? The answer is simple. It's called self. Our selfishness gets in the way of making wise decisions. Look closely at this verse and it will help you understand:

> He who leans on, trusts in, and is confident of his own mind and heart is a [self-confident] fool, but he who walks in skillful and godly Wisdom shall be delivered. (Prov. 28:26 AMP-CE)

To walk in wisdom, you sometimes have to put what you feel like you want to do aside. The wonderful thing is that with God's help you can. Listen to this regarding the heart of someone who is choosing to walk wisely with God:

> And the Spirit of the Lord shall rest upon Him—the Spirit of *wisdom* and *understanding*, the Spirit of *counsel* and might, the Spirit of *knowledge* . . . and obedient fear of the Lord. (Isa. 11:2 AMP-CE, italics mine)

Isn't that beautiful!

As followers of God and believers in his Son, Jesus, we are given the Holy Spirit to help guide us through life in *all* wisdom, understanding, and knowledge. You have the Holy Spirit in you to help you know what to do in every situation and for all the decisions you have to make.

Remember that wise guy Solomon? Here is what he had to say in Proverbs chapter 8:

> Do you hear Lady Wisdom calling?
>> Can you hear Madame Insight raising her voice?
> She's taken her stand at First and Main,
>> at the busiest intersection.
> Right in the city square
>> where the traffic is thickest, she shouts . . .
> "Don't miss a word of this—I'm telling you how to live well,
>> I'm telling you how to live at your best." (vv. 1-3, 6)

Lady Wisdom is that voice inside you, the Holy Spirit, whom you can hear at times speaking to your heart, whispering things like:

*Don't do that.*

*Don't buy those shoes; you don't have the money.*

*Don't send that text with those angry words.*

*Don't go out with that guy; he is not a wise person.*

What Solomon was saying is this: Wisdom is calling out. It's right there for you to hear. It's not hidden, it's not secret, and it's available to you at every crossroad and intersection of your life. And if you will listen to it, your life will be blessed!

It's like my story about the television—I could hear wisdom calling out, but it was my choice whether to listen and respond to the direction and guidance being given to me.

Wisdom calls out to us through many different ways, not only by the voice of the Holy Spirit but also through the Word of God. One of the easiest ways to grow in wisdom is by reading and studying God's Word. The Bible is the book of wisdom! Just reading one chapter a day from the book of Proverbs can give you insight into how to handle life's decisions wisely. One of the things I love to do is to read Proverbs from *The Message* version of the Bible. It is full of helpful hints about life and making good and wise choices.

Another way to grow in wisdom is by surrounding yourselves with wise people.

> Become wise by walking with the wise;
>> hang out with fools and watch your life fall to pieces.
> (Prov. 13:20)

That's a pretty clear picture, isn't it?

It might be that you need to think about who you are hanging around with and listening to. Are they wise? Honestly, it is unwise for any of us to hang around with and be friends with foolish people. And it is unwise to have foolish girls as your best friends.

At church this morning during the worship and prayer time, I turned to the two girls behind me and asked them to pray for me. I told them I needed God to help me with this chapter on wisdom. I shared with them how I had been working on it for days and struggling to write what was on my heart. As my friend prayed out loud for me, she said, "God, please help Debbie to ask for wisdom and believe that you will give it to her." That was it! I was writing a chapter on wisdom, I knew my favorite verse on wisdom by heart, and I had asked people to pray for me, but I had not actually stopped and personally asked God to give me wisdom to write about wisdom! So today I did just that. I prayed and asked God to give me wisdom to write this wisdom chapter. And I believed he would!

That, my friend, is the thought I want to leave you with: the Bible says when you ask God for wisdom, you have to believe he will give it to you.

Remember James 1:5? After it tells us to ask for wisdom, it goes on to say this. (Pay attention, because it's really important!)

> But when you ask [for wisdom], you must believe and not doubt, because the one who doubts is like a wave of the sea, blown and tossed by the wind. That person should not expect to receive anything [any wisdom] from the Lord. (vv. 6–7 NIV, brackets mine)

God wants to give you wisdom, but more than that, he wants you to trust him and believe in your heart that when you call on him for help, he will do what he promises to do.

Maybe, as you're reading this, there is an area of your life where you desperately need help. Perhaps you have made some foolish decisions, spending money you didn't have or making commitments you couldn't keep. Or maybe you lied about something, and now you feel stuck. It could be you need help and wisdom with a friendship, as a wife, or in your parenting.

Maybe right now, in this moment, you realize the challenges you are experiencing are a result of your unwise choices, and you want to believe that God can help you and give you wisdom to know what to do from here. Or maybe you just want to keep growing in your understanding of walking with God and learning to make wise decisions in everything you do and say.

No matter where you find yourself today, God wants to help you. Just ask him to give you wisdom and then believe that he will, and he will do it! He promises you that!

Here is a prayer you can pray:

*Dear Heavenly Father,*

*Thank you that you care about every detail of my life and that you want to help me make wise decisions in every situation I face. I believe you want to guide me and show me how to walk in wisdom every day I live. I ask you to give me wisdom for what I am facing today. I need it! You've said that if anyone asks you for wisdom, you will generously give it. So I ask you to help me know what to do regarding _____. Help me not to make a foolish decision but to listen to your voice and follow it.*

*By faith, I believe that you can and you will show me what to do.*

*Amen.*

# BELIEVING . . .

## Affects Your Mind and Spirit

I pray that God, the source of hope,
will fill you completely with joy and peace
because you trust in him.
Then you will overflow with confident hope
through the power of the Holy Spirit.
(Rom. 15:13 NLT)

# *Nine*

## You Have an Attitude

Put on your new nature, and be renewed as you learn to know your Creator and become like him. (Col. 3:10 NLT)

at•ti•tude: the mental position you choose to take toward life, circumstances, and people

It's your attitude, so it's your decision
whether you want to keep it or not.

This was not good. I could feel the inside of me starting to boil and my face getting hot. And it wasn't even a hot day! It was actually a very cold day in the middle of January, so it wasn't the temperature that was causing me to overheat (and no, it wasn't a hot flash, smarty-pants). I couldn't blame it on a fever, because I was feeling fine physically.

No, the heat I was feeling was not related to my physical well-being; it was connected to my heart and soul. The embarrassing truth is that John had said something I didn't agree with, and I'd made the decision to dwell on thoughts I shouldn't have. Now I had an attitude of the wrong kind.

It wasn't even caused by a big issue or a yelling fight (or should I say *disagreement*—I'll admit we've had a few of those). In all honesty, I don't even remember what I was frustrated about, and it was only last month! But I do have a problem. It's called prideful, selfish thinking. I like to be right and I like to win. So does John. Whoever said opposites attract was not at our wedding!

So on this day, just because I wanted John to agree with my opinion, I went from singing "Oh Happy Day" to wanting to throw a plate. Okay, that's a bit of an exaggeration. Maybe.

It all happened so quickly. In about five seconds flat, I allowed the thought of "I am right!" to transform into negative feelings and emotions, and I went from happy to angry. I made the decision to have a bad attitude, and the only thing that was going to change it was if and when John came to his senses and decided that I. Was. Right.

If you are human and breathing, you have probably experienced a plate-throwing mood. Maybe you are even in the middle of a bad-attitude day right now. It's not too fun, is it? Thankfully there are ways to learn how to maintain a good attitude in life (besides persuading everyone to always give in to your opinion and do things your way).

Over the years, I have learned how to deal with my emotions and bad attitude more quickly and effectively than I did thirty years ago. So on that day in the middle of my confrontation with John, when my angry thoughts finally came up for air, I stopped and said a prayer. *God, help me with these feelings. I know they are not of you and they are not what you desire for me.* With his help, I made the decision to change my attitude right then and there. In an instant, as I humbled myself and purposefully changed my thinking, the burning and churning inside my soul began to subside. Now, don't tell John I said this, but I still think I was right (even though I don't remember what I was right about!). But that, my friend, is irrelevant. Instead of proving I was right, I chose to focus on adjusting my thinking and my attitude to line up with God's will for me in that moment, and the overwhelming feelings of wanting John to see that I was right began to subside.

Years ago, when John and I were first married, God used a verse to help me in this "I want to always win and be right" struggle. This same verse came to my mind again that day. Many times these words have been the key to saving me from letting my attitude run wild and cause more damage to my day, my marriage, and my life.

*Do nothing* from fractional motives, [through contentiousness, strife, selfishness, or for unworthy ends] or prompted by conceit

118

and empty arrogance. Instead, in the true spirit of humility (low-liness of mind) let each regard the others as better than and superior to himself [thinking more highly of one another than you do of yourselves]. Let each of you esteem and look upon and be concerned for not [merely] his own interests, but also each for the interests of others. (Phil. 2:3–4 AMP-CE, italics mine)

And don't miss this:

Let this same attitude and purpose and [humble] mind be in you which was in Christ Jesus: [Let Him be your example of humil-ity] (v. 5 AMP-CE).

Darn it, that verse convicts me every time. It hits me right where it hurts. That part about doing nothing out of fractional motives, selfishness, or unworthy ends (like wanting to win) makes me think God must have said, "Put that part in there just for Debbie. She's going to need to read it pretty much once a week or more." And my guess is that I am not alone on this one, that you have had your bad-attitude, stop-annoying-my-life moments too. But you don't have to admit it. Not yet.

Attitude. It is the mental position you choose to take toward life, people, and circumstances. I sometimes wish it wasn't *my* attitude, particularly my bad attitude, that causes me problems. I wish I could blame it on someone or something else, such as John, the weather, being tired, or being female (we girls love using that excuse). But I can't use any excuse or blame anyone for my attitude, because it's mine—mine to own and mine to control. I choose my attitude—nothing gives it to me but me!

The longer I live, the more I have come to understand how important a person's attitude is to their walk with God, their well-being, and their everyday life. Attitude is more important than anything you do or say, because it is the rudder that guides and directs what you do and say. Your attitude has the power to make or break your day. It can strengthen or destroy your relationships. It can bless or curse your home, your children, your marriage, your job, and your hopes and dreams for the future. It has the power to rob you of hours, days, months, years, and even a lifetime of peace, hope, and joy. Attitude affects absolutely everything.

Right now, at this very minute, my attitude choice can affect what I am doing. It can help motivate me and encourage my soul to believe God is leading me as I write these words to you. Or it can discourage my soul and cloud my perspective and make me incapable of believing that God is with me. To be honest, I have to constantly battle my thoughts to keep my attitude in line with what I know is right. Attitude, for me, is a daily and nightly choice.

It's interesting how I notice a huge difference in my productiveness when my attitude is in alignment with my faith and trust in God. When I choose to focus my mind and thoughts on walking in faith, my attitude is optimistic, and that motivates and inspires me to look at anything I am trying to accomplish through the eyes of faith. When my attitude is filled with doubt or negative thoughts toward people or situations I am facing, I am easily frustrated and discouraged, and my attention can start to focus on myself and my own ability.

There's much about life we can't change. We cannot change the past, who our parents are, or where we are from. We cannot change the people around us (the negative girl at the office, the mean girl at school, the cranky neighbor) or the fact that people will fail and disappoint us. We cannot change the weather, the time, or the opinions of others. There are so many things we cannot humanly control. But we do have control of what is most important, and that is our attitude toward everything we cannot control. In a very powerful and miraculous way, your attitude affects all of those things you cannot change, because it changes you. When you have the right attitude, the world around you and the circumstances you are facing look different. It's like a rainbow in the storm clouds of life.

Did your mother ever say to you, "Get rid of your attitude"? I know I said it to my kids. When you think about it, it's really a silly command, because getting rid of your attitude is impossible. We always have an attitude. We just don't always have the right one.

Listen to this:

> Since you have heard about Jesus and have learned the truth that comes from him, *throw off* your old sinful nature and your former way of life, which is corrupted by lust and deception [selfishness]. Instead, let the Spirit renew your thoughts and *attitudes. Put on* your new nature, created to be like God—truly righteous and holy. (Eph. 4:21–24 NLT, brackets and italics mine)

Just in case we try to use the old "you make me mad" excuse for having a bad attitude, God put these verses in the Bible just for us.

You pick your attitude. No person or situation can give you a bad attitude. Nice try, sister, but that just isn't how it works.

In the Bible is a story about two guys who were beaten and thrown into prison for their faith. Their names were Paul and Silas, and they were evangelists who traveled around and told people about Jesus. During their missionary journey, they experienced much opposition from those who didn't want to hear their message. When their ministry began to affect and disrupt the town because of miracles occurring and people being converted to Christ, they were seized by angry citizens, accused of causing trouble, and ultimately arrested by the town rulers. The officials tore off Paul's and Silas's clothes, beat them with rods, threw them into the inner prison (the deepest, darkest, dirtiest corner), and clamped their legs in irons.

Now, I don't know about you, but I think I might have been struggling with my attitude right about then. *Come on, God. I was working for you, I was sacrificing for you, I was telling people about you. I was even doing miracles in your name. What's the deal?*

I might have, of all things, tried to blame God for my bad attitude. But not Paul and Silas. These guys were amazing! I so love and admire their spirit. Get a load of what they did in Acts chapter 16, verse 25:

> About midnight Paul and Silas were praying and singing hymns to God. (NIV)

You may need to read that again. Those two guys were real people just like you and me. They were in a lot of pain. They were mostly naked and lying on the floor of a filthy prison cell. They hadn't done anything sinful or illegal. They could have been frustrated and even angry. But Paul and Silas weren't complaining or whining or yelling at the guards. They weren't curled up in a ball on the prison floor, moaning about their situation. They were praying, singing out loud, and worshiping God.

Wow, what an attitude!

Paul and Silas didn't let their situation affect their message or their hope or their mood. In the middle of being treated horribly, while they were still physically hurting from being beaten and in chains for doing nothing wrong, they were singing praises!

When I read this, I have to admit I am convicted, and my prayer is, *God, please help me! That is so how I want to be.*

What chains or challenges do you find yourself in today? Most days, if you are anything like me, you come up against situations that can trigger negative thoughts, feelings, and emotions that require you to make an attitude choice, and you will have to decide what mental position or attitude you're going to take in response to your circumstances.

You may be facing a difficult situation as you read this.

Maybe you are having difficulty in your marriage.

Maybe your husband isn't a believer and he is hard to live with.

Maybe your adult children are unkind to you and don't respect you like they should.

Maybe your boss is hard to work for and you feel you are treated unfairly.

Maybe you are walking through a financial crisis.

Maybe you are in prison for something you did or even didn't do.

Maybe things are just not going your way and life is extremely difficult right now.

Everyone walks through trials. Some are big and some are small. We all have the option of how we are going to respond to those trials. So what attitude do you want to have?

Whether you choose to have a singing attitude or a stinky attitude, that affects not only you but also the people around you. People are watching how you respond to life and the challenges you are facing. And if you are only thinking of yourself, you will stink.

Paul and Silas chose to sing, and it changed everything. Was it their praise that changed their attitude or their attitude that caused them to sing? Who knows. I would imagine they didn't really feel much like singing. But with faith and believing hearts, they did anyway. And their attitude of praise, in the middle of their challenge, opened doors of blessing and opportunity.

> Paul and Silas were praying and singing hymns to God, and the other prisoners were listening to them. (Acts 16:25 NIV)

*The Message* puts it this way:

> The other prisoners couldn't believe their ears.

I bet not! They had probably never heard anything like it before.

The joyful, believing attitude of Paul and Silas was noticed by the people around them. Look at what happened next.

> Suddenly, there was a massive earthquake, and the prison was shaken to its foundations. All the doors immediately flew open, and the chains of every prisoner fell off! The jailer woke up to

see the prison doors wide open. He assumed the prisoners had escaped, so he drew his sword to kill himself. But Paul shouted to him, "Stop! Don't kill yourself! We are all here!"

The jailer called for lights and ran to the dungeon and fell down trembling before Paul and Silas. Then he brought them out and asked, "Sirs, what must I do to be saved?" (vv. 26–30 NLT)

I can't help but wonder if that jailer was one of the men who had brutally beaten Paul and Silas with rods, or if he might have been the one who had thrown them in the cell and put them in chains. Either way, he was involved and responsible for the challenges and difficulties they were experiencing that day. But their decision to praise God in the middle of difficulty changed this man's life and the lives of his entire family.

While writing this chapter, I've been feeling so convicted about the times I have allowed my circumstances to affect my spirit. It makes me wonder who is watching me. Who has seen me when I've had a stinky, faithless, ungrateful attitude? And if instead I had been singing, would they have heard me, and could it have changed their lives?

Who is watching you? Who is noticing how you respond to the situations you are in today? Your friends, your family, your children, your unsaved husband, your mean boss, your cranky neighbor, the inattentive server at the restaurant, the girl in line ahead of you taking too much time?

Here is another saying to remember: "Life is 10 percent what happens to you and 90 percent how you handle what happens to you." So true! How you choose to handle life's situations affects your life and everyone else who is watching you.

Your attitude is the inner thoughts of your soul, which feed your actions. But an attitude can be hidden from view until it is revealed by your actions. You can have a sinful attitude and nobody may know except you. But if you don't deal with it, I promise eventually it will come out. A self-centered attitude will eventually show itself by building you up and tearing others down. A stubborn attitude will be revealed through a spirit of disobedience or defiance instead of gentleness, humility, and a servant's heart. Stinking thinking and actions are really a matter of the soul. To put it bluntly, a bad attitude reveals a selfish, faithless, unbelieving spirit.

Romans 12:2 says,

**Do not conform to the pattern of this world. (NIV)**

Simply put, don't let the circumstances of the world around you cause you to act like or be something you shouldn't. There are no circumstances you face or people you come in contact with that have the power to dictate your attitude or your actions.

Verse 2 goes on to urge us to "be transformed by the renewing of your mind"—by a new attitude. In other words, you can choose to change your attitude by hitting the refresh button of your mind. Right now, in this moment, you get to decide whether you are going to sing or not.

When I was in my teens, during the summer I attended the Spencer Lake Youth Camp in Wisconsin. I remember sitting in chapel every morning on the weathered, hard wooden benches, surrounded by hundreds of other campers my age. The leader would start our day by yelling enthusiastically into the microphone, "Attitude check!"

And with that, all of us would respond by yelling back, "Praise the Lord!" at the top of our lungs. This seemingly insignificant routine was repeated three times every morning for the entire week of camp. It was really a simple challenge reminding us to pay attention to our attitudes and to keep praising God in every situation.

I still find myself repeating that cheer in moments when I am tempted to have a bad attitude. I mentally walk up to the microphone and yell, "Attitude check!"

Am I allowing the actions of people to upset me? *Attitude check!*

Am I allowing the circumstances surrounding my life to discourage me? *Attitude check!*

Am I allowing any hurt and pain I'm walking through to cause me to despair? *Attitude check!*

Changing your attitude takes faith to believe God is with you and that he is going to help you. Changing your attitude takes thankfulness, along with being grateful for others and for all God has done for you. Changing your attitude takes action—choosing to sing and praise God in the middle of whatever you are walking through.

There may be people in your life who are making bad choices that are hurting you or your family. You may be in emotional pain or physical pain from disease or sickness. Or you may just have let someone or something get under your skin like a splinter, and now you are having a rotten-apple day. You may think there's nothing that can change how you feel.

The answer is simple. God's Word says there is something you can do right now that will bring joy and sunshine into the room and into your heart. All you have to do is make the decision by faith to tell your soul to sing. And that, sweet girl, will change everything, because it will change you!

> Rejoice in the Lord always [delight, gladden yourselves in Him]; again I say, Rejoice! (Phil. 4:4 AMP-CE)

So go ahead—I dare you to change your attitude, start praising, start singing, and watch what happens next!

# *Ten*

# Peace Is Not Always Quiet

I am leaving you with a gift—peace of mind and heart. And the peace I give is a gift the world cannot give. So don't be troubled or afraid. (John 14:27 NLT)

**peace:** a state of calm and tranquility, free of chaotic, frantic, unsettling thoughts and emotions

Peace is not found in a life void of the noise
and chaos. It is when, at the center of
everything, there is a calm and quiet soul.

*eep . . . beep . . . beep.*
*Oh no!* The warning sound broke through the peace
and quiet of what had otherwise been a fairly calm day.
As I stood in the mudroom, I scrambled to find my keys so I could
push the burglar alarm stop button on my key chain.

I knew it was only seconds before the gentle beeps switched
to a full-on alarm, signaling the police department and everyone
within a mile of our garage that there was a potential emergency
at the Lindell home.

*Where are those keys?*

I dumped the contents of my purse and watched as everything
spilled out—small change, lip gloss, used Kleenex, receipts, Advil,
and my wallet.

But no keys.

I looked at the security pad, desperately racking my brain for
help. (That part of the brain that is supposed to remember pass-
words and codes—I don't think I have it.)

What was the code? 1-2-3-4? Nope. How about my birth date?
Nope. Phone number? Nope. *Ugh! Just praying for protection
would be so much easier than this!*

Then I had a thought. *I must have left my keys on the seat of the car.*

I scrambled back into the garage and opened the car door, and there they were . . . but it was too late. The gentle warning sound of *beep . . . beep . . . beep . . .* was now a blaring, ear-piercing, cover-your-ears-and-run *BEEP! BEEP! BEEP!* alerting everyone within miles that there was a burglar in the neighborhood (and that was me).

My heart was now racing. My forehead was dripping sweat. My normally low blood pressure was no longer low. And in an instant, I had an "I can't believe this is happening" headache. Well, so much for my calm, quiet, and peaceful day! It was nothing serious, just an alarm going off, yet it not only took the quiet away but stole my peace of mind too.

I don't know about you, but I am not too fond of those anxious, stressful, chaotic feelings that zap my peaceful heart. Or those times when I feel a bit out of control, and my fairly calm and controlled life turns upside down and nothing goes like I wish it would.

An unexpected bill shows up in the mail. *Goodbye, peace!*

Your preschooler has a meltdown, screaming at the top of her lungs in the cereal aisle of the grocery store, and everyone stops to watch. (You know that "can I please just go hide behind the Fruit Loops" feeling?) *Goodbye, peace!*

You back out of a parking space, all happy and smiling, thinking about the shoes you found on sale, when all of a sudden you hear a horrible, dreadful sound. Your car bumper has just met someone else's. *Goodbye, peace! Goodbye, smile.*

Your boss walks in with his "I'm not too happy with you" face and says that he needs to meet with you, "now!" *Goodbye, peace! Hello, stomach churn.*

And here's my own personal favorite. Once, when I was cheerfully and excitedly unpacking boxes in the back bedroom of our newly built home (it was moving-in day), I smelled smoke. I went running down the hall and around the corner to see my kitchen filling up with smoke. True story! I'd set a pastry box on our new stove (my excuse was there was not another open spot on the counter), and somehow a burner had been turned on. And now the apple pastry was on fire and my newly installed, white cabinets were totally black. Goodbye to that cheerful "I'm excited to be moving in" feeling. Hello to that stressful "open all the windows," "turn on the fans," "I hope John doesn't get back here with the truck anytime soon" feeling! Thankfully it was only minor damage. Whew!

Okay, now it's your turn. What was your last "try to steal my peace" moment?

Peace, that tranquil, easy-breezy state of mind. Ah, yes. We all want it. And we all desperately want to live surrounded by it twenty-four hours a day, enjoying calm seas. But how is it even possible in a fast-paced, stress-filled, get-it-all-done, make-it-happen world, where our kids have meltdowns, bosses get upset, and kitchens catch on fire? We all know exactly what it is like to lose our peace of mind. It can be something big, like a fire in the kitchen, or something as small as setting off your own security alarm—and in an instant, your life goes from fairly calm and peaceful to that chaotic "where is Jesus when I need him?" feeling.

The closest friends of Jesus, his disciples, knew exactly what it felt like for life to go from peaceful one moment to stressful the next. One calm evening, their quiet and relaxing boat ride across the Sea of Galilee suddenly became very stressful. And the crazy thing was Jesus was right there in the boat with them.

One of the most memorable places I've ever been to is the Sea of Galilee in Israel. This is the part of the world where Jesus spent much of his time as an adult, ministering and traveling from town to town along the coastline with his disciples. This sea is actually a large freshwater lake about thirteen miles long and eight miles wide, surrounded by a mixture of beautiful green landscape, rugged hills, rocky shoreline, and small towns and villages. Most of the time the water is calm and clear like glass. But that calmness is known to change suddenly, due to the mountainous terrain on the eastern end of the coastline, which can create very strong winds and even violent storms. On the day the disciples lost their peace, that is exactly what happened.

The story unfolds in Mark chapter 4.

> He [Jesus] went back to teaching by the sea. A crowd built up to such a great size that he had to get into an offshore boat, using the boat as a pulpit as the people pushed to the water's edge. He taught by using stories, many stories. (v. 1, brackets mine)

You get the idea that the crowds were so big they were gradually pushing Jesus closer and closer to the edge of the water. He must have thought, *I'll just get in a boat.* Good thinking, Jesus! And it was there that he taught the people with his disciples until late in the afternoon. I would imagine the disciples spent the day trying to help Jesus—getting him water when he was thirsty, finding him a snack when he was hungry, and managing the crowds of people trying to listen. By afternoon, they were probably all feeling pretty tuckered out.

> He said to them, "Let's go across to the other side." They took him in the boat as he was. Other boats came along. A huge storm came up. Waves poured into the boat, threatening to sink it. And Jesus was in the stern, head on a pillow, sleeping! They roused him, saying, "Teacher, is it nothing to you that we're going down?" (vv. 35–38)

Let's stop a minute and imagine what it would have been like for the disciples. The boat they were in wasn't exactly a yacht. It would have been a very simple wooden fishing boat, about twenty-five feet long, seven feet wide, and four feet deep, powered by a sail. They had probably fished together many times in this particular boat, but today it was an escape ferry and a haven, giving a very weary Jesus and his friends a break from the crowds as it slowly made its two-hour journey to the other side of the lake.

Everything seemed calm. Jesus, exhausted from teaching all day, found a place to lie down in the back of the boat and fell asleep. The rest of the disciples were cruising along, probably chatting about the day, maybe discussing all the stories Jesus had told. It all sounds so . . . well, peaceful.

Suddenly, without warning, billowing darkness descended on them in the middle of the stillness, and what seemed like the mother of all storms enveloped their little fishing boat. One translation of the Bible says the storm that came was "of hurricane proportions" (AMP-CE).

So there they were, stuck in the middle of the biggest storm they had ever seen. It might help you to know that they were very familiar with sailing on this lake. They had probably grown up swimming in it. And they were experienced fishermen. They had seen storms come and go. But their experience was no match for this night; this storm was different.

Huge waves were crashing down over them. Pouring rain pelted down on their faces, making it impossible for them to see. The strong and swirling wind tossed their boat like a child's toy and shredded the sail to pieces. Booming claps of thunder echoed out over the sea. Powerful bolts of lightning crashed around them, illuminating the swirling dark clouds above.

This was like nothing they had ever seen. It was chaos . . . and they were terrified!

There was no escaping the storm's madness, there were no life jackets, there was no radio to call for help, and there was no place to hide from the danger that had suddenly descended upon them.

I can envision those fishermen drenched in sweat and churning seawater. I can hear them screaming and yelling over the wind, rain, and thunder as they frantically grabbed on to whatever they could to keep from being thrown overboard. They most likely thought they were going to die. I don't know if I can think of many things more frightening (except for something related to heights, that is).

The Bible doesn't say how long the storm lasted or how long it took the seasick fishermen to decide to wake up Jesus and announce to him that they were going to die! That's right, I bet you almost forgot that Jesus was there, fast asleep on a pillow in the back of the boat.

Stop reading for just a minute. I want you to imagine a space twenty feet away from you and think about Jesus being there, curled up asleep. (Now, that's a funny thought!) The point is, there in the middle of that violent storm, in the midst of the disciples' panic, the lightning, and the rain, Jesus was at the most just twenty feet away from them . . . sleeping.

Why wasn't he awake helping them? Could it be that Jesus knew that everything was going to be okay? Hmm, there's a novel idea.

Finally, one of the disciples must have thought, *We need to wake up Jesus!* (That is even funny to say. "Wake up, Jesus!") With that, through the lightning and against the wind and rain, he crawled over to Jesus.

Can you just picture that disciple shaking Jesus and screaming at him above the sound of the storm? "Jesus, wake up, we're going to die! Don't you care?"

Mark tells us this about that scenario:

He arose and rebuked the wind and said to the sea, Hush now! Be still (muzzled)! And the wind ceased (sank to rest as if exhausted by its beating) and there was [immediately] a great calm (a perfect peacefulness).

He said to them, Why are you so timid and fearful? How is it that you have no faith (no firmly relying trust)?

And they were filled with great awe and feared exceedingly and said one to another, Who then is this, that even wind and sea obey Him? (vv. 39–41 AMP-CE)

The disciples had forgotten one thing. It didn't matter what was happening around them. It didn't matter if it was stormy or calm. Jesus was there. Their hearts could be at peace, because even asleep, Jesus was in control of the boat and the storm.

I want to ask you something. What takes away your peace? Right now, wherever you are, stop and close your eyes for a moment and let your mind imagine the most peaceful setting you can think of.

Did you do it? What was your thought?

Did you picture yourself floating across the sky through fluffy clouds in a hot-air balloon (which I will probably never do)? Or sitting on the bank of a quiet stream with a fishing pole? Or nestling on a corduroy sofa with a fluffy blanket and big mug of hot chocolate and marshmallows in front of a crackling fire on a snowy day? Or—one of my favorites—walking barefoot on a sugar-white, sandy beach, watching the sunset to the sound of rolling waves?

It's interesting, but I would guess that whatever you pictured, it was not something that was noisy or crazy-busy. Isn't the mind wonderful? In a split second, it can transport you from where you are to somewhere quiet and peaceful. But I hate to interrupt your peace and quiet. You can't stay up in that hot-air balloon forever. Life will eventually bring you back down to earth.

Most of the moments of our lives are not characterized by peace, quiet, and stillness. At least, not where I live. And probably not where you live either, unless you walk on the beach every day without a care in the world. At every season, there are challenges, decisions, pressures, deadlines, newborns, teenagers, college bills, job hunting, aging parents, and unexpected stresses of all kinds.

My world rarely, if ever, represents a tranquil place where turquoise waves splash against a pristine beach. My life is filled with a constant array of challenges to my inner peace. Life's surprises interrupt my quiet and threaten to steal the stillness God desires for my soul. If I'm not careful to guard my heart from worry and chaos, they can become the norm.

Fortunately, having a quiet spirit with peace ruling your heart is not contingent on the circumstances of your day. If so, it would be impossible to achieve. The beautiful thing about a quiet, peaceful spirit is that it can be felt and enjoyed in the midst of craziness, challenge, and even chaos.

Psalm 46:10 says,

Be still, and know that I am God. (NIV)

It sounds like we can choose to have a quiet heart, right? That we can know the peace God offers us in every situation.

When Jesus was sleeping in the boat that day, he was big enough to handle the storm, and he wanted his disciples to believe and trust that he was. Remember, he asked them this *after* rebuking the storm: "Why are you so timid?" In other words, "What took your peace away? How is it that you have no faith, no trust in me?"

Here is another way to look at what Jesus was saying:

No faith + No trust = No peace!

It is interesting to note that on the very night the disciples found themselves panicking because of a storm, they had spent the day listening to Jesus telling stories for hours about who he was. And in the days and weeks before, they had seen him do miracle after miracle and had heard him teach on trusting in him. He had told them, "Don't worry about your life and don't be anxious about the future. I am big enough to take care of everything that concerns you."

I want you to hear this, my friend. This is for you today. God wants you to know and understand that he is big enough to handle everything in your life. But for you to live with a heart that is at peace and rest, you have to believe he is!

Isaiah 40 says this:

> Have you not been paying attention?
> Have you not been listening?
> Haven't you heard these stories all your life?
> Don't you understand the foundation of all things?
> God sits high above the round ball of earth. (vv. 21–22)

God, your God, is a big God. Let's stop for a second and think about the universe he created, the one we live in.

The distance in miles between the earth and the sun, at its closest point during the year, is . . . 93 million miles! How crazy is that number? But it gets even crazier. The distance from the sun to the center of our galaxy is 30,000 light-years (a light-year is 6 trillion miles). To travel across our galaxy, the Milky Way, you'd have to go 100,000 light-years! And get a load of this—the Milky Way has 100 billion stars, and that's not counting all the other galaxies. Yet God calls every one of those stars by name.

And to think, he holds this all together!

Did you say, "Wow"? Because I just did.

Just this week as I was writing this chapter, scientists discovered *another* planet and named it Kepler-452b. God's creation is so big and so vast that we will never be able to explore it all. It is altogether awesome and beyond belief.

Understanding the greatness of God—that he created the universe, the galaxies, the planets, the stars, the sun, and the earth—helps us to live life with a peaceful heart and to trust and believe that he can take care of every situation we face. It doesn't matter how big or how small the problems are that are taking your peace away and bringing stress and worry into your life. The key is knowing how big your God is. Nothing is too difficult for him.

Jesus said this:

> I have told you these things, so that in Me you may have [perfect] peace and confidence. In the world you have tribulation and trials and distress and frustration; but be of good cheer [take courage; be confident, certain, undaunted]! For I have overcome the world. [I have deprived it of power to harm you and have conquered it for you.] (John 16:33 AMP-CE)

You will have some challenges and even troubles in life, but you don't have to lose your peace, or any sleep either, for that matter. God gave you the gift of his peace, and it is free for you to take advantage of, day and night.

Not only does God have your back, sweet girl, but he is in front of you as well, and on top of that he even knows what tomorrow will look like. You do not need to be afraid of anything. Any storm. Any person. Any "the end of the world is near" announcement. Any newscast. Any weather report. Any doctor's test. Any terrorist threat. As a believer in the truth of God's Word, walking by faith in what his Word says, you can trust and not be afraid or anxious. You can have peace in your heart and mind.

Now, that doesn't mean you act fearless or stupid. If you run out onto the highway, you are probably going to be hit by a car. If you put your hand in a fire, you are going to get burned. If you drive a hundred miles an hour, you will hopefully get a ticket. If you don't take care of yourself, you will eventually get sick. So there is a right kind of fear to have that protects you from harm. That is a good and healthy fear.

Feeling fear does not necessarily mean you don't have faith. God designed us to naturally respond to danger with fear for our protection. It was natural for the disciples to fear when they faced that terrible storm. What is important is how you respond to the fear—whether you respond with trust and believe God is with you, or you doubt God, panic, and don't believe he is going to take care of you. The problem with the disciples was they lost hope that Jesus would be able to take care of them in the storm.

It's my opinion that worry is the biggest enemy of our peace. Face it, as girls, we are worrywarts. But it doesn't help one teeny, tiny bit to worry about anything. Listen to Jesus' words in the book of Matthew:

> Therefore I tell you, stop being perpetually uneasy (anxious and worried) about your life. . . . Who of you by worrying and being anxious can add one unit of measure (cubit) to his stature or to the span of his life? . . . But seek (aim at and strive after) first of all His kingdom and His righteousness (His way of doing and being right), and then all these things taken together will be given you besides. So do not worry or be anxious about tomorrow. (6:25, 27, 33–34 AMP-CE)

Worry is a result of not trusting. Worry is a stealer of peace. Worry doesn't help you deal with anything. And worry that is not dealt with destroys faith and becomes sin. If you find yourself constantly worrying, you honestly need to repent and ask God to help you stop. You may have to do that over and over again. But as you make it a priority to turn your worrying into walking by faith, you can and will change your habit!

Maintaining a peaceful heart also means cultivating a quiet spirit by renewing your mind through God's Word and creating the right atmosphere around you. It means creating the right environment in your home, your car, and your life for the peace of God to be welcome. These are good questions to ask yourself: *Is the presence of God welcomed in my home? Have I created an environment where peace can thrive?*

I want those who enter our home to sense God's peace—including John and myself! When you walk into our house, the first thing you'll see is this message painted on the wall of the entryway:

> May the LORD bless you and protect you.
> May the LORD smile on you and be gracious to you.
> May the LORD show you his favor and give you his peace.
> **Numbers 6:24–26**

I love looking at those words. They are a visible reminder to John and me that the peace of God is available for us to walk in every minute of every day. But having a Bible verse about peace painted on the wall does not guarantee peace will be present. I've been in homes where there were Bible verses on display in every room and yet the atmosphere was not at all peaceful. You still have to make the choice to walk daily in the peace that God offers.

The words you allow yourself to speak are important too. Words have power. If you find there is strife and discord everywhere you go, you might need to take a look at yourself and what is coming out of your mouth. When you find your thoughts and words are out of control, you have to decide to control them. No one else can do that for you. Not even God. He can give you the tools to walk in peace and provide you with all the help you need, but only you can make the decision to change from worry to faith and begin speaking faith-filled words.

> Let the peace (soul harmony which comes) from Christ rule (act as umpire continually) in your hearts. (Col. 3:15 AMP-CE)

Living in God's peace is a choice. Once you know God, he offers you the gift of his peace, and you are the one who controls whether you live under the umbrella of it or not. No storms, no circumstance, and no person can steal it from you. Life will never be totally quiet, but it can be filled with peace, God's wonderful peace!

I leave you with this thought, based on Isaiah 26:3–4:

Your God will guard your mind and keep you in perfect and constant peace when you commit yourself to him, lean on him, and hope and confidently believe in him. So trust and believe in the Lord forever, for he is your everlasting Rock. He is your peace!

# Eleven

## Treasures in the Darkness

"Oh, he even sees me in the dark!
   At night I'm immersed in the light!"
It's a fact: darkness isn't dark to you [God];
   night and day, darkness and light, they're all the
   same to you.

Psalm 139:11–12, brackets mine

**dark•ness:** when your eyes cannot see; concealed, mysterious, and hidden

God did not intend for you to endure
the darkness but to dance under the stars
that are hidden there.

There is something magnificent and almost breathtaking about a clear, midnight sky. Hidden behind the light of day are hidden treasures to behold—treasures we would never see without the darkness. I think God put them there—those little twinkling jewels called stars—to remind us that whenever the lights in our lives seem to go dim or even go out all together, we need not fear because treasures are there for us to find. Beautiful secrets await that will only be found in the dark times of our lives.

"Be home before dark!"

You most likely heard that phrase, or something like it, as a child. If you are a mom or a grandma, you would probably agree with that directive. In the darkness, there are things unknown. In the darkness, you cannot see clearly. In the darkness, you can get lost.

Darkness is scary and sometimes bad, right? I don't know about you, but that is what I grew up thinking.

When I was around ten years of age, everything I had learned about the darkness seemed to catch up with me. So, as most children do, I went through a period of time when I was afraid of all the things that came to life in the dark. I was especially concerned at night in the bedroom I shared with my little sister, Susie. We had matching twin beds that were pushed up against the wall on either side of the room, with a window in between. Even though I wasn't alone at night, I was still very afraid of what might be lurking in the shadows of my room. My ten-year-old thinking told me that darkness had unwanted secrets. They could be hiding in the closet or, even worse, under my bed, where they would come out and grab me after I was asleep.

To calm my anxiousness (and keep from getting nabbed by the darkness monsters), I came up with a plan. During the day, when the hot-pink and yellow daisy wallpaper was lit up by the sun, I would practice running down the long, narrow hallway, past my parents' and brother's bedrooms, and catapult myself from the doorway onto my bed. As I jumped, I would flip the light switch next to the door. It seemed much safer if my feet did not touch the floor. I actually got quite good at this and could manage the leap with only one foot touching the creaky wooden floor. And just in case, I had a secret weapon tucked under my pillow. If needed, my dad's heavy-duty black flashlight with the yellow on and off switch was ready to zap the darkness.

Whether intended or not, as we walk through childhood, the things we are taught about darkness subtly instill in us that it is something we may need to be afraid of and avoid. Did you learn any of these?

- Use a night-light.
- Every flashlight should have fresh batteries.
- Always be home before dark.
- Never be out alone in the dark.

Over time, our minds begin to believe that when any form of darkness comes into our lives, it signifies something that is bad, filled with unknowns, danger, and evil. Of course, that view is not totally incorrect. We all understand that bad things happen in dark alleys and that sin in the Bible is described as black and dark. And we would all agree that the invention of the lightbulb was a wonderful thing for everyone (thank you very much, Mr. Edison!).

Light is necessary to living. We need it to see the beauty of color. We need it to reveal what is happening around us. We need it to keep from getting lost and to show us the way. We need it to find our car keys, cell phone, and contact lens that we dropped on the floor. Sunlight keeps us warm and makes the trees, flowers, and plants grow. Light is very important and downright valuable to everyday living!

But God didn't just make the light; he made the darkness too. Now, there is an interesting thought. At the beginning of time, God created light to illuminate what had already been there—the darkness. That light is essential for showing off his creation and a necessary component of our existence on earth.

Genesis 1:3–5 says this:

> God spoke: "Light!"
>     And light appeared.
> God saw that the light was good
>     and separated light from dark.
> God named the light Day,
>     he named the dark Night.
> It was evening, it was morning—
> Day One.

Those words are so incredible! They describe the moment when, for the very first time, light ate darkness for breakfast. The Bible says that before God created light and made the day, the earth was formless and empty, with darkness covering the deep. The universe was without any light, and God was just hanging out there in all of his glory. And then (drumroll, please) out from the dark emptiness, by his creative power and might, God changed everything when he said, "Let there be light!" In an instant, light illuminated the blackness.

Can you imagine that? Brilliant, vibrant, perfectly created, wondrous light crashing into the deep, black darkness of nothing. Even God had to think that moment was pretty awesome. Maybe he even stopped a second and thought, *Wow! Look at what I just did.*

God outdid himself. And I am so thankful he thought light was a good idea. But—are you ready for this?—so is the darkness! Have you ever wondered why God, for his very first act in creation, didn't choose to do away with darkness altogether? Why he chose to create the black night sky? Why he divided the night from the day and gave darkness its own place in space to reveal and display its character? You might need to sit and think on that one for a few minutes. I did.

God didn't have to keep darkness. He could very well have shouted out into the emptiness, "Let there be light—and no more darkness," eliminating darkness completely and permanently. But he didn't. God purposefully chose to keep it, give it a place of importance, and even give it a name. And in doing so, he revealed that darkness, the absence of light, was not to be viewed as a negative; instead, it was intended for good. God applauded and reveled in everything he made at creation—even the darkness.

> And God saw everything that He had made, and behold, it was very good (suitable, pleasant) and He approved it completely. (Gen. 1:31 AMP-CE)

God loves the darkness of night as much as the light of day. (If you live in Alaska, you said "Amen" to that!)

My daughter, Savannah, came by the house the other night, and as she walked into the kitchen, her first words were, "Mom! Have you been outside tonight?" Her tone was dramatic and insistent. She grabbed my arm and began pulling me toward the back door. "You need to see this!"

I gave in, and arm in arm, we walked out onto the patio and into the night. "Look up!" she said.

Her enthusiasm was contagious. I wondered what I was going to see. At first I couldn't see much of anything, the glowing haze from the lights I'd left behind obscuring my vision. But then, as my eyes and my mind adjusted to the clear, moonless night, something amazing began to happen. Out from the darkness, across the sky, a thousand treasures came dancing into view.

"Look at all the stars, Mom. Aren't they incredible?"

For a few minutes, the two of us just stood there staring in wonder at the sky. Like diamonds displayed on a gigantic black velvet canvas, in the middle of the darkness of night, the twinkling stars revealed their brilliance right before our eyes. I will never forget it, because it was the first time I realized and understood that the God who made the light made the darkness too. It was designed and purposed by him to reveal things to us, hidden treasures only found in its blackness.

On that night, I was still recovering from breast cancer and a double mastectomy. I was in the middle of walking through my own personal darkness journey. Yet standing there under those stars, I heard God whisper, *No matter how black the darkness or how empty the night, I am always there, ready to share my hidden treasures with anyone who is willing to look up.*

The Bible talks about how walking through a trial is like walking through a dark night. But God is there.

> Even when I walk
>     through the darkest valley,
> I will not be afraid,
>     for you [God] are close beside me.
> (Ps. 23:4 NLT, brackets mine)

> "Oh, he even sees me in the dark!
>     At night I'm immersed in the light!"

> It's a fact: darkness isn't dark to you;
>> night and day, darkness and light, they're all the same
>> to you. (Ps. 139:11–12)

I just love those verses. They are so comforting. Think about it! Even when you are walking through dark times, whether you are facing loneliness, heartache, pain, sorrow, despair, fear, or sadness, God is right there. He has not left you to walk through the darkness on your own. He is not hiding. He is not distant. He is not surprised by it. He is actually right there next to you, filling your darkness with his presence.

Our human nature urges us to run hard and fast away from any and every challenge and difficulty. Who on earth would ever choose to go through a difficult or dark time? Not this girl. I'd almost always prefer calm, comfort, bright sunshine, and seventy-five-degree days. And while we're dreaming, we might as well go all out. I'll take a white sandy beach, a lounge chair, an umbrella, and a pink lemonade slushy. And how about a golden tan to top it all off? (That would be a dream, because my nickname is Snow White.) Go ahead! Close your eyes for just a minute and use your God-given imagination. Can't you just smell that beachy, saltwater air? Feel the soft breeze? Hear the waves? Taste the icy, tart pink lemonade? *Ah, this is nice.*

Now, if you're actually reading this on some gorgeous beach, I am so happy for you! Be sure to post a pic on Instagram and tag me so I can see what the rest of us are missing.

Okay, back to reality. We both know life isn't all sunny days on the beach with ice-cold lemonade. Not every day is bright and clear. Some days are downright overcast with darkness ahead. We have all experienced nights and days that were very difficult.

It seems counterintuitive for us to believe that darkness can be good—to wrap our human thinking around the idea that not only sunny days but also dark ones hold hidden treasures that are meant to bless us and reveal God's beauty. But listen to these verses:

> I will give you the treasures of darkness and hidden riches of secret places, that you may know that it is I, the LORD, the God of Israel, Who calls you by your name. . . . I form the light and create darkness. (Isa. 45:3, 7 AMP-CE)

I want you to notice two fascinating things here. First, God calls the darkness a treasure. Second, look at the word *hidden*—it's an interesting word. When something has been hidden, often it has been obscured from view on purpose. God likes to hide things—like surprises in the night. For reasons we may not clearly understand until we get to heaven, God has hidden beautiful and valuable treasures for us to find in our dark valleys and difficult times. When we're in the middle of the dark and we can't see or feel our way forward, God wants to reveal precious and valuable things to our hearts. It's as if he is saying, "Look out into the night, sweet girl. I have some twinkling stars I want to show you."

I love that!

When you are facing darkness, he has not disappeared or forgotten you. He has not relinquished his will and plan for you. He is with you! And he is still right there beside you. Why? you might ask. Why are there times of darkness in our lives? Isaiah tells us God's answer to that question:

> That you may know that it is I, the LORD, the God of Israel, Who calls you by your name. (v. 3 AMP-CE)

When I'm walking through a trial, I find myself calling out to God more than ever for help. I want to hear him and feel his presence and know he is there. And it is there in the dark, when everything else is unclear, that my ears are more aware of him whispering my name, saying, *Debbie, I am with you, even though you cannot see ahead or understand how things are going to work out. I know who you are, precious girl. I know your name.*

That is why the psalmist says,

> Even if I go through the deepest darkness,
> I will not be afraid, Lord,
> for you are with me. (Ps. 23:4 GNT)

It is why the apostle Paul writes from prison,

> Let us exult and triumph in our troubles and rejoice in our sufferings. (Rom. 5:3 AMP-CE)

It's why James tells us,

> When troubles of any kind come your way, consider it an opportunity for great joy. (James 1:2 NLT)

God is in the darkness of prison, pain, suffering, difficulty, and discouragement. He does not leave us to walk in the dark alone.

Can we stop here for a second? Maybe today *you* are experiencing a difficult trial, and it feels very, very dark around you. Maybe you feel like you are desperate for some light to help you find your way out of a situation or circumstances. Don't despair. God is right beside you, my friend. Just hold out your hand to him, and he will reveal hidden treasures and secrets to you that will encourage your heart.

It's important to understand that sometimes the difficulties or darkness we are facing is because of our own foolish, sinful, and selfish choices. Those times when we refuse to listen to God's Word and the leading of his voice, when we determine to do our own thing no matter what the consequences are. It is in those times that we are left groping in the darkness of sin for a way back to God's presence.

But even the darkness brought on by our own sinful decisions carries its own hidden and valuable treasure. Stay with me, because this is pretty amazing. *Even that lightlessness of walking in sin is a gift and a treasure from God.* It's a darkness that reveals to a spiritually lost person their need to call on God for help and to search for the treasure of his salvation and forgiveness.

Isaiah said this about what Jesus would do when he came to rescue and redeem the darkness of people's hearts:

> The people who walked in darkness
>   have seen a great light.
> For those who lived in a land of deep shadows—
>   light! sunbursts of light! (9:2)

It is when God opens the eyes of those walking in sinful darkness that they can see and experience his radiant light of grace and forgiveness. So the darkness of sin is a backdrop that brilliantly reveals the greatest treasure of all—Jesus. He is the only light that breaks through the darkness of sin.

> Everything was created through him;
>   nothing—not one thing!—
>   came into being without him.
> What came into existence was Life,
>   and the Life was Light to live by.
> The Life-Light blazed out of the darkness. (John 1:3-5)

So even for those who are living in sin, whose souls are filled with darkness, there is a treasure waiting to be found. The light of the Savior is there to lead them back to his grace and salvation.

The thing I want you to see is that when you are walking with God, darkness isn't all bad. Everyone will experience days that are dark and difficult. Everyone walks through trials and battles the darkness of sin. The important thing is to trust in God, look to him, and believe that he is still there. He hasn't left. The darkness doesn't hide him. Instead, the darkness reveals him all the more!

If you are alive and breathing (and you are!), you have probably concluded, like I have, that trials are a part of life and you shouldn't be surprised by them when they come. Some are short-lived and others are more challenging and take longer to pass. Trials will come. That is not a faithless statement; it is just the truth. God doesn't want us to run from them; he wants us to embrace them when they come, because there are good things hidden in the trials of life.

> When troubles [dark times] of any kind come your way, consider it an opportunity for great joy. For you know that when your faith is tested [in the dark], your endurance [your faith] has a chance to grow. (James 1:2–3 NLT, brackets mine)

You can't run from the darkness. Trying to outrun darkness is like trying to outrun the setting sun. You can't escape difficult times, and honestly, as strange as it sounds, you wouldn't want to.

This past year I found out how true this is when I walked through my own journey in the darkness. One day in particular, I was lying on my bed, the window shades were up, and the sunlight of a fresh spring day was dancing between the baby leaves fluttering in the breeze. All of the brightness and light from outside seemed to make every corner of the house glow. Yet the light seemed to stop at the foot of my bed. It was as if the cream-colored sheets and blankets that had surrounded me for the past two months had hardened into an impenetrable shield, keeping the light away and sealing in the darkness. At least, that was how I felt.

As much as I wanted to, as hard as I tried, I could not change the landscape in my mind. Darkness was there, it seemed to be slowly creeping in everywhere, and I was beginning to have difficulty seeing anything clearly.

That January I had been diagnosed with breast cancer. Within a week of my diagnosis, after a string of doctor appointments and consultations, it was determined that due to the challenges of my breast anatomy, I would need to have a double mastectomy. It may sound funny to say this, but that was the easy part. As I sat and heard the doctor's words, I determined to trust and believe that God was with me, and as I did, I felt his supernatural peace surrounding me. I was confident that if he didn't choose to take the cancer away, he would help me through the surgeries and the process of recovery.

I did have moments of wondering what those would be like and of processing the emotions of losing that part of my body, but I wasn't afraid. I went into the first surgery with an expectation that everything would be okay. Even in the days following surgery, in spite of multiple unexpected complications, I was sure that I would be up and around and back to normal in no time.

When I questioned them about my recovery time, the doctors had assured me that although it was a "big" surgery, I should be feeling well enough to go back to work part-time within two or three weeks. But that wasn't the case. So there I was, nearly eight weeks later, dealing with seemingly endless complications, discomfort, and physical weakness. I didn't care one bit about having boobs anymore. All I wanted was to be up and around. I missed life! I wanted to be back to normal!

After weeks and weeks of little to no progress in my recovery, it didn't feel like I was walking through the valley. Instead, I felt like I was lying in a very deep, dark pit with no emotional or physical energy to find my way out. I began to struggle with a myriad of anxious thoughts. *What if I never heal? What if I am sicker than the doctors think? What if I have cancer somewhere else? What if I feel this way forever?* The darkness of anxiety, fear, discouragement, and doubt began to creep into my soul.

During those days, even though I believed God was there, I knew I needed more than ever to reach out to him to steady me and to focus my mind on the truth of his Word. So that is what I did. Night after night and day after day, I would rest my phone next to my pillow and listen to worship music and the Bible being read to me. It was through a determination to trust in God's Word and listen to the whisper of his voice calling my name in the night that I was able to rise above my despair.

Even though that journey was more physically painful and emotionally challenging than anything I had ever walked through before, God revealed himself to me in very intimate and beautiful ways that I will never forget and would not trade for anything. When I couldn't get up out of bed, when I couldn't do anything on my own to make things better, when I couldn't see the future—that was when I had nothing else to look to but God. It was then that I realized more than ever that without him I am nothing. He is my life, my breath. He is my everything!

Here are some of the hidden treasures you will find in the darkness.

*Darkness makes you listen more closely to God's voice.* When you can't see, you listen. And I did. In the night, when I was in pain, when I couldn't get comfortable, when I couldn't sleep, I listened and he whispered my name over and over and over again, reminding me of these words:

> I will give you the treasures of darkness and hidden riches of secret places, that you may know that it is I, the LORD, the God of Israel, Who calls you by your name. (Isa. 45:3 AMP-CE)

*Darkness causes you to desire his comfort and peace.* The peace of God is a treasure that becomes more valuable in the darkness. That peace makes it possible to say, "I will fear no evil, because he is with me." It is soothing, like a soft and fuzzy blanket wrapped around your weary shoulders.

*Darkness builds your faith and trust.* I know for a fact that my faith is stronger today than it was before that journey. I am closer to Jesus than ever before. And I have a greater faith to believe that he will never leave me alone in the dark—because he didn't!

Even though I prayed for healing and believe that God can heal (because I have been healed before), and even though I know that in an instant he could have said to the cancer, "Be gone!" and it would have been, that is not what happened. Even though I trusted God, my trial didn't go away in an instant. My constant pain didn't just disappear. The discouraging thoughts didn't instantly vanish and become a non-issue. God had a different journey for me—one that caused my faith to grow like never before. Remember James 1:2–3? Those verses say that trials make our faith stronger, and that is so true.

*Darkness reminds you of the value of faith-filled friends and family.* I am abundantly blessed to have a husband who was there to love and care for me. Through our dark journey, John and I became more aware than ever of the need to have believing friends and the value of being a part of a caring, loving church family.

*Darkness teaches you that things aren't really that important.* When I was sick, I could have cared less about a dollar bill or a new pair of shoes. The only thing I desired was God's presence. That became even more important to me than getting well. I thought about heaven every day and understood in a deeper way how this earth is not my home. When you think that way—which we should every day—things become . . . well, nothing, really.

*Darkness is where you learn to care for others.* One of the most wonderful things that happened during my cancer journey is how it gave me a deeper understanding and empathy for others. What a gift! I have a greater compassion for people who are walking through physical challenges and pain or those watching their family members face them. I have a different perspective of what it means to face cancer, the frustration of not being well and of not having an answer, and the battle with depression and discouragement. And I now know how to pray, love, and care for others in a way I didn't before.

157

*Darkness is often where new dreams and ideas are birthed.* It is interesting to think that babies grow in the darkness of the womb. It seems to me that similarly, it is in our dark times that God births new dreams in our hearts. During my sickness, I received fresh ideas of how I could lead others better and serve and encourage girls who are walking through difficulty, sickness, and discouragement. A new ministry called Sisterhood Cares was birthed in our church. It is flourishing, and in just one year, it has touched the lives of hundreds of women and their families.

As you can see, God revealed lots of hidden treasures to me in my darkness. Now I believe more than ever that darkness is not all bad!

In other words, don't be surprised to find a treasure when you are walking in the dark. God has some special secrets for you there. I promise that if you just look up, you will see stars shimmering in the blackness of the night—bright shining stars that God has hidden there just for you.

If you are walking through a dark time, I want to pray for you. If you are not, would you just pause a minute and pray with me for the girl holding this book in her hand who desperately needs this prayer?

*Dear Heavenly Father,*

*I may not know the name of the precious girl who needs these words today. But you do! You love her, and you are right there with her in this dark moment of her life. You understand what she is feeling. You see right where she is at. You know her fears, and you care about what she is facing. I pray that in this moment, faith will rise in her heart so she will believe your Word, and that even though she cannot see clearly ahead, she will hear you whispering her name. I pray that she will seek you with all of her heart and that you will reveal beautiful treasures to her. Help her to look up. Help her to see the beauty of your presence in the middle of this night. Help her to take your hand and let you lead her to the light that is ahead.*

*Amen.*

Now, remember, sweet girl, Jesus says this to you:

I am the world's Light. No one who follows me stumbles around in the darkness. I provide plenty of light to live in. (John 8:12)

He is all the light you need, even in the dark.

## *Twelve*

# Big Girls Do Cry

You keep track of all my sorrows.
  You have collected all my tears in your bottle.
  You have recorded each one in your book.

Psalm 56:8 NLT

**tears:** drops of clear liquid that flow from your eyes

There are some words
that only tears can speak.

tried to stop them. There did not seem to be a good reason for them to fall. At least, I didn't think so. I wasn't at the dentist, I wasn't watching a sad movie, I wasn't in pain, and I wasn't cutting up an onion for vegetable soup.

Instead, I was being pampered by my hairstylist. She was giving me a little head massage to the tune of soothing spa music. As hard as I tried, I could not hold them back, and one by one they came in a slow, trickling parade down my face. Thankfully the room was dimly lit, and since nothing I did (like pinching my leg or changing the channel in my brain) seemed to stop them, I just let them do their dance down my face and hoped Cory would think the dabbing of my eyes was due to water splashing on my cheeks.

Why was I crying? It didn't take much thought for me to figure it out, but I didn't want to admit the reason to myself.

Four months had passed since I had heard the words, "Debbie, I am sorry to tell you this, but it's not good news. You have breast cancer." As you know, my recovery from surgery and treatment was a very slow journey, but I was now back on my feet and gaining strength. Yet the emotions from the long months behind me were still fresh, and when touched, they reacted. Just like the nerves that were still healing under my skin, my emotions were revealing to me that they were healing as well.

The day after I was diagnosed with breast cancer, I'd been in this same room with the same music, enjoying the pleasure of the same relaxing atmosphere. Strangely, I didn't cry that day. But today I did. I sat there and analyzed the reason for my tears, and I came to the conclusion that the only reason I was crying was just because I needed to. It wasn't because I was emotionally weak or discouraged or down in the dumps. The truth was I needed to cry and that was okay.

Ever been there? Are you crying now? If you are, that's all right. I actually have a lump in my throat as I write this, and my glasses are fogging up. I am thinking about you and the emotions you might be facing today that are possibly causing you to feel the need to cry. If I was there with you, I would hand you a tissue, look you in the eyes, and say, "It's okay. Big girls can cry."

It's interesting to me that for some reason, when we graduate from childhood to adulthood, there is a subtle or at times a very obvious perception that comes with "maturity," and it goes something like this: big girls shouldn't cry. I disagree with that 100 percent! Maybe that's because, over the last few months as I have walked through one of the most difficult times of my life, it seems like I have cried a lot.

Last April I was speaking to a group of about 2,500 women. The auditorium was filled with females of all ages. I asked them to raise their hands if they had cried for any reason that day. I was a bit shocked when over half the audience raised their hands. In that moment, it was like there was a mutual sigh of relief. *Oh, good, there are other grown-up girls who cry.*

As I was researching the scientific facts on tears, I was reminded of how much I loved biology in school. I especially enjoyed studying the human body, including drawing and labeling the specific parts we were studying. (As I recall, the only time I got an A on a biology paper was when it was a drawing. Hooray for all the artsy types out there!)

In my research, I discovered some amazing things about tears. Did you know your body started creating your own tears when you were just fourteen days old? And within a few short months, your eyes began to shed tears to express frustration when you wanted out of your crib or when you were angry at not being fed on time. The truth is that you and I were born to cry. Yippee! We are not weird.

Science is now shedding light on the differences in the way men and women cry, and why. It appears that women are uniquely designed to shed more tears than men because our tear glands hold less moisture, so tears build up and spill out more readily. In general, a woman cries four times more often than a guy, for an average of 5.3 teary days a month.[1] (If you are a guy and you are reading this, no comments allowed!)

Scientists have identified three distinctly different kinds of tears. Although most of us don't shed tears every day, our tear ducts produce a thin, salty film over the eyeball called *basal tears*. Every time you blink, these tears flow across your eyes to keep them moist and free of dust and other irritants. Basal tears also carry antibodies to defend against unwanted bacteria. So basal tears are continuously cleansing your body of harmful things. If the eyes are the window to the soul, maybe tears keep our souls free of harmful things too.

The second type of tears is *reflex* or *irritant tears*. When something irritates your eye, reflex tears flood out to fight it off, as well as any other intruders, such as insects, sand, onion juice, and contact lenses.

While I believe tears were made in heaven, I do not believe contacts were. Several weeks ago, I was on my way to meet the girls from the office to get pedicures and then have lunch together. As I drove down the highway, my right eye began to burn and then water uncontrollably. By the time I pulled up to Jessica's Nails, my left eye was the only one working. My right eye was squeezed shut, gushing a flood of tears, and causing a great deal of pain. Thankfully one of my friends came to my rescue. As the tears poured down my face, I was able to pry my eyelid open long enough for her to assess the cause. She looked, then gasped, "Debbie! There is a wadded-up contact sticking out from your eye!"

"What? You have got to be kidding me!" It was crazy. The last time I had tried to put a contact in that eye had been weeks ago. It was a good thing my eye ducts were working, cranking out those reflex tears and forcing that lost and wrinkled contact to flee. It made me very appreciative for those tears that work tirelessly to flush harmful and unwanted things out of my eyes.

Now, besides basal and reflex tears, we also produce *emotional tears* (what an appropriate name!). These are the tears that emerge when our emotions become overcharged with intense sadness, overwhelming compassion, or even joy and laughter. Emotional tears carry hormones and other toxins accumulated during times of stress that our bodies need to eliminate. They can also stimulate endorphins, the body's natural painkiller. Is that not the coolest?

Emotional tears help calm us down, stabilize our moods, and lower our heart rate. When stress chemicals in our bodies accumulate and build up to toxic levels, weakening the immune system, it is then that emotional tears come to the rescue, reducing the chemicals and discharging proteins associated with physical pain.

Tears are just one of the many miracles that work so well that we take them for granted. Even though at times we want to be quick to wipe them away and hide the evidence, God has a different view of tears.

This past year as we were packing to move, I decided to take the oversized glass jar out of my closet. It was filled with mostly pennies, along with a few nickels, dimes, and quarters that had accumulated over the years. It was very heavy. Some of the coins had been dug out from under the cushions of the couch; others had been rescued from the pockets of my jeans or the bottom of the washing machine. Each little coin was valuable, and now I was going to find out how much this jar of coins was worth.

My mom and I decided to guess how much money was in the jar before hauling it to the grocery store coin-counting machine. I guessed $45 and she guessed over $100. I thought she was way off, but she wasn't. When the noisy machine finished processing all the coins, there was $119.54! Wow, now that was worth saving!

Just like that jar filled with valuable coins, God saves each one of your tears and stores them in a bottle. I can just picture the tear storage warehouse in heaven with rows and rows of shiny glass jars. On the outside door of the warehouse is a sign: "Caution—Priceless Tear Storage."

There in Section L is my bottle with my name on it. Inside it holds every single tear I have ever cried.

The tears I cried as a teenager on my front porch steps when I found out my grandma had just died from a heart attack.

The tears I cried with my neighbor and friend as we said goodbye and she and her family backed out of their driveway for the last time.

The tears I cried as a sleep-deprived mom who was trying to do her best raising her children.

The tears I cried in frustration and pain during my recovery from breast cancer surgery.

The tears I cried with my daughter-in-law when her father passed away unexpectedly.

The tears I cried with my daughter when she broke up with her boyfriend.

The tears I cried as I prayed over you while writing this book.

It is amazing to think that every last one of those tears is precious to God. I can just imagine him lovingly inspecting the bottles of tears he has stored. He asks the warehouse manager, "Are they being carefully cared for? These are precious to me. Be sure they are looked after. I don't want to lose any of them."

Listen to the words in this verse in Psalm 56:

> You keep track of all my sorrows [difficulties].
>> You have collected all my tears in your bottle.
>> You have recorded each one in your book. (v. 8 NLT,
>> brackets mine)

Big girls do cry, and that's okay. Whether your tears come from a big reason or a little reason or a reason you can't begin to understand, you are not alone. Your Heavenly Father knows you personally, is personally there with you and for you when you cry, and cares about each and every tear.

One of my favorite stories in the Bible is about a woman who cried. She cried for a very good reason—she loved Jesus and was brokenhearted at the thought of losing him. After he was crucified and buried in the tomb, she was sure that he was now gone from her life forever.

Of all the resurrection stories the apostle John could have told in his Gospel account, he started with this one. And of all the people Jesus could have chosen to meet on that resurrection Sunday, he chose a woman who was crying. Her name was Mary Magdalene, and according to the Bible, she was a woman with a very imperfect and sinful past.

Mary's eyes were brimming with tears as she visited the tomb. She was so overcome with sorrow and sadness that she talked to angels like it was normal!

> They [the angels] said to her, "Woman, why are you weeping?"
> She said to them, "Because they have taken away my Lord, and
> I do not know where they have laid Him." (John 20:13 NASB,
> brackets mine)

Overcome by loss, drowning in tears, Mary was unable to process the supernatural things that were happening before her very eyes. From her vantage point, heaven was indifferent, she had been abandoned, and Jesus was nowhere to be found.

Most of us have been there—overwhelmed, feeling alone, our eyes a fountain relieving the pressure we feel inside. Maybe that's where you are today, but don't miss what happens next. Mary turned around and saw Jesus standing there, but John 20:14 tells us that she "did not know that it was Jesus" (NASB).

The ever-present Savior, the one who said, "I will never leave you or forsake you," was there beside her. Think of it. On that first resurrection morning, there were a thousand things Jesus could have been doing, a thousand people he could have been visiting, a thousand sermons he could have been preaching, but he chose to spend time with a woman who was crying.

"Mary," Jesus said to her. He said her name, because just knowing he was there with her and for her was all she needed.

Emotions are a unique part of the human design and are usually viewed as specific and intense psychological and physical reactions to what we experience in life. Crying is just one of the many options for displaying what we are feeling. Yet it is true that even though we were created to show our emotions and express how we feel toward events and people, untamed emotions can get out of control and get us into trouble.

Last week we were with our one-and-a-half-year-old granddaughter, Henley. She is the cutest little munchkin (and I want to make it known that people say she looks like me). As a baby, she was so mellow she put her brothers to shame with her easygoing and seemingly calm, laid-back personality. But somewhere around the age of one, she began to understand how she could use her emotions to make people aware of what she was not happy about and to try to get her way. The emotional response she happens to be using a lot these days is screaming, crying, and screaming (that part I do not think she got from me!). Her mother is aware that this will not work for Henley long term, so she is working to help her understand that there are appropriate emotional responses to different situations.

Emotions are from God, and just as he created Henley with emotions and the ability to display what she is feeling, he did the same for you. Jesus himself experienced lots of emotion. In our desire to be like him, we can often forget that emotions are a part of who he is. On earth, he felt and showed compassion often. He was angered by sin. He was troubled by hurting people. He was deeply moved and hurt by the actions of sinners. He wept when his friend died, seeing the sadness of the family. Yes, Jesus even cried.

And big girls cry too.

Being an optimist, hopeful and confident about the future, means typically exhibiting strength and a positive outlook during difficult times. But when sorely challenged, even an optimistic person can buckle under discouragement. The truth is my hope for the future, or even for this day, must be grounded in something other than my own strength of personality or stamina, or it will ultimately fail when tested.

> [Now] we have this [hope] as a sure and steadfast anchor of the soul [it cannot slip and it cannot break down under whoever steps out upon it—a hope] that reaches farther and enters into [the very certainty of the Presence] within the veil. (Heb. 6:19 AMP-CE)

Is that not the most reassuring verse you've ever heard? It tells us that we do not ever have to rely on our own strength of personality or optimism to stay hope-filled and tearless. Our souls can be securely fastened to a steadfast and unshakable anchor of supernatural hope . . . and his name is Jesus. No matter what happens, no matter what we are walking through, no matter what plans don't go the way we expected, our anchor, our hope, our *Jesus*, will always be our strength!

So if you feel like crying today, that's okay. Just like with Mary, the God who knows you personally is personally there for you, to care for you, gather up your precious tears, and put them in your bottle.

And I have more good news for you. When you and I get to heaven, we will never cry again!

> God will wipe away every tear from their eyes; and death shall be no more, neither shall there be anguish (sorrow and mourning) nor grief nor pain any more, for the old conditions and the former order of things have passed away.
>
> And He Who is seated on the throne said, See! I make all things new. (Rev. 21:4–5 AMP-CE)

So, sweet friend, if you are crying tears today, just remember this: Jesus did too, and he is right there with you, whispering your name and saying, "Everything is going to be okay."

# BELIEVING . . .

## *Makes Being Together Even Better*

You were all called to travel on the same road
and in the same direction, so stay together,
both outwardly and inwardly.
(Eph. 4:4)

# *Thirteen*

# You've Got a Friend in Me

Love from the center of who you are; don't fake it. Run for dear life from evil; hold on for dear life to good. Be good friends who love deeply; practice playing second fiddle. . . . Get along with each other; don't be stuck-up. Make friends. (Rom. 12:9–10, 16)

friend•ship: relationship, companionship, harmony, giving of yourself; sharing your heart and life with another

Friends are like flowers. They come
in all shapes, sizes, and colors. To enjoy them
close up, you just have to pick one.

Today is a morning filled with sunshine, and you and I are going to meet for coffee at the corner café. It's an adorable little place where we love to sit and chat. It is so cute inside, with every detail friendly and inviting. The cozy room is filled with cream-colored wooden tables for two with a vase of fresh flowers on each.

I'll get there a few minutes ahead of you and order your favorite coffee or tea. Mine is always the same—a grande nonfat latte in a big, white ceramic cup.

This place is tucked away near the center of town in an old brick building on a quaint little street filled with shops. On the right side of the café is a little bookstore, and on the other side is an adorable, shabby chic boutique with the cutest outfit on display in the window. We might have to do a little shopping later.

On the front of the café are two huge windows framing a bright teal-colored door with a bell that jingles to welcome everyone who enters. Just inside the door sits a glass case filled with antique cake stands of all different levels piled high with scrumptious, freshly baked pastries. You can smell the deliciousness as soon as you walk in. My favorite one is the peaches and cream cheese Danish.

I'll go ahead and pick out a couple for us to share. We are not counting calories today.

When you come in, I'll be sitting at the corner table by the paned-glass window. It's quiet there, and we'll be able to sit, talk, and laugh together as long as we want. I've blocked out a couple hours, and I can't wait to see you and catch up on what has been happening in your life.

How fun! Just so you know, I am smiling at the thought of meeting you there.

It is my hope that as you read the words in this chapter, you will realize that *you have a friend in me, even though we may never have the opportunity to meet in person.*

Friendship. What a beautiful idea. God designed us to need and want to have life-giving and faith-strengthening relationships with other girls. He wants us to be embracing of one another, encouraging, supportive, kind, loving, and thinking about the needs of others over ourselves. If we all decided to be the kinds of girlfriends that God intended us to be, there would be an abundance of beautiful and life-giving friendships for us all. And that would make the world a better place!

The Bible tells us how to be a true friend to others. It begins with understanding how Jesus wants to be your friend. Actually, he wants to be your very best friend. Listen to what he says in John chapter 15:

> This is my command: Love one another the way I loved you. This is the very best way to love. Put your life on the line for your friends. You are my friends when you do the things I command you. I'm no longer calling you servants. . . . No, I've named you friends. (vv. 12–15)

Did you catch that? Jesus wants to be your friend! Just stop and think about that for a minute. Not only does he want to be your friend, but he is also the most perfect, loving, and caring friend you could ever imagine having.

Friendship should always begin with Jesus. One of my favorite verses says,

> Watch what God does, and then you do it, like children who learn proper behavior from their parents. Mostly what God does is love you. Keep company with him and learn a life of love. Observe how Christ loved us. His love was not cautious but extravagant. He didn't love in order to get something from us but to give everything of himself to us. Love like that. (Eph. 5:1–2)

With that verse as the baseline, I want to talk about a few basic aspects of friendship that I believe will be an encouragement and help to you as you process the kind of friend you want to be.

*Friends are all different.* I love this saying: "Girlfriends are like flowers—they come in all different colors, shapes, and sizes (and even perfume scents)." Even though we are probably very different from one another, Jesus loves you and he loves me, and he calls both of us his friends. He does not have prequalifying guidelines for what kind of person he chooses to be friends with. He loves people. And because of his love for people, he wants to be friends with everyone. His love for people is completely unselfish, and he embraces and accepts all who come to him.

That is how we should be toward others. It doesn't mean we have to be best friends with every girl, but it does mean we should love and care for every girl who comes into our world and that we should want to treat each one like a friend.

*The quality of friendship is not determined by the length of time you've known someone.* You can know a person for a short amount of time and sense a mutual and beneficial bond that was neither expected nor sought out. Less than two years ago, through this book project, I met a girl who quickly became very dear to me. I shared many personal things with her and asked her to pray for me. When I met her, I had no idea of the physical issues I would be facing. But as I walked through them and our friendship grew, I found out that she had gone through a cancer journey with similar complications. She does not live near me, and we have been together in person only one time. But we had what I would call a heaven-planned connection. God wanted us to meet. He wanted us to be friends who would encourage each other at this moment in our lives.

*Friendship is not defined by proximity and closeness.* A friendship can continue even when you're miles apart and rarely, if ever, see each other. The girlfriend I mentioned above lives hundreds of miles from me, but I still call her my friend. And I have friends through social media whom I have never even met. They encourage me, bless me, ask how I am doing, and pray for me. Don't ever underestimate the power of these types of friends. The apostle Paul wrote letters all the time to people he did not know and called them his friends. That is why when I tell you I consider you one of my friends, I don't say it flippantly. I view you as part of my sisterhood!

*Friendship is not confined to those with similar interests, social status, or age.* I have found those things have little or nothing to do with whether or not I can experience a life-giving relationship with someone. One of my dearest friends is my neighbor Kate. She is fifteen years younger than me, with three young children; I am a grandmother. She doesn't like to cook; I love to. She is a marathon runner; I am *not*. (Side note: I am praying her crazy amount of energy will rub off on me and that in my next book, I will be able to tell you a story of how I ran alongside her in a half marathon, kept up with her, and ultimately beat her by a fraction of a second. Ha!)

*Friendships can vary in length of time.* Not all friendships last forever. Some friendships last for years. Some may even span your entire lifetime. But others will be there for a season, and then, for various reasons, that friend or group of friends might move on and even move completely out of your life. That does not always mean something bad happened. Everything has a season, even friendship.

*Sometimes friends have to go.* There may be a time when you have to choose to end a friendship because that person or group of people is not helping you live a life that is honoring to God. Sometimes you lose friends simply because they misinterpret your motives or don't understand where God is leading you. Years ago when I first felt God speak to my heart about changing the philosophy and direction of the women's program in our church, I was so excited! What I wasn't prepared for was how some of my closest friends, who I thought would come alongside to encourage and support me, voiced disapproval. I was already fearful of stepping out into the unknown waters of a new level of leadership, and now I was losing some of my dearest friends. It was hard. When God calls you to step out in faith, or when you grow deeper in your commitment to him, some of your friends may not understand or be supportive.

This happened to people in the Bible too. Abraham left his family and friends when, by faith, he followed God's leading to a new land. Moses had to deal with being misunderstood and ridiculed by the people he was trying to lead. Joseph tried to explain to his older brothers what God had told him, and they became jealous and actually sold him into slavery over it. (I would encourage you to read Joseph's story if you are going through a time of being misunderstood in your faith or feeling abandoned by family and friends.) And there were many more, including David and Paul. They all lost friends because of their commitment to do what God was calling them to.

If you've experienced losing a friend because of a misunderstanding regarding what you are committed to, you know how hard it can be. But whenever God calls you to do something for him or to respond in obedience to his Word, do not let the voice of a friend—any friend—cause you to back away or keep you from doing what he wants you to. If that ever happens—and it may at some point in your life—remember not to look down on that friend for not understanding. Sometimes friends grow apart and must travel different paths. And if you choose to keep loving them, your paths just might come back together in the future.

*Friends have power.* Don't underestimate the power of a friend. They can strengthen you or tear you down. First Corinthians 15:33 says,

> Evil companionships (communion, associations) corrupt . . . good manners and morals and character. (AMP-CE)

Proverbs 13:20 says,

> Walk with the wise and become wise, for a companion of fools suffers harm. (NIV)

The friends you choose to walk close to affect you, not just in your actions but in your spirit as well. Friends can push you toward God or pull you away from him. They can inspire goodness and growth or tempt you to go back to a lifestyle that you know is sinful and wrong. They can influence what you believe, discourage you from being in church, or steer you toward bad habits. Simply put, they just may not be good for you during a particular season of your life. Your willingness to sever a friendship may be the best thing you ever do to strengthen your relationship with God. It also just might be the trigger prompting your friend to evaluate where they are in their walk with God and to make changes in their life. You can have friends who don't know Jesus or who struggle with sin, but they cannot be your closest friends. You have to make sure you are the one influencing them and that they are not influencing you.

Please hear me on this: it's not wrong for you to withdraw from a friendship. If a friend is causing or tempting you to sin or to not follow God with all your heart, you need to back away from that relationship.

*Friendships will come in varying levels of closeness and intimacy, and that is a good thing.* You can handle only so many close friendships. And those you are closest to should be very carefully chosen. I recently saw an Instagram post of a pack of lions and this caption: "Surround yourself with those who are on the same mission as you." It's a perfect motto for how you should select your close friends. They are the girls in your world who understand that your mission in life is to love God with all your heart, and they support and strengthen you in doing so.

In the Gospels, you can read about the life of Jesus when he was on earth. You can see he loved people of all walks of life, including sinners whom he shared meals with, talked with, and welcomed to follow him. He also had many other friends, both men and women, who came alongside him, traveled with him, and encouraged him in all he did. They supported him in life and helped him to fulfill what he was called to do on earth. However, his closest friends were carefully selected. His twelve disciples shared in ministry with him, and within that group were three whom he confided in more than the others.

The point is, you need to be careful and selective about who you choose to spend the most time with. If a person is not strengthening your life and leading you closer to Jesus but is pulling you further from him instead, they should not be your best friend—and maybe not even a friend at all.

Listen to what Proverbs 12:26 says:

> The righteous choose their friends carefully,
>   but the way of the wicked leads them astray. (NIV)

*Friendship is made. It doesn't just magically happen.* You've heard the saying "If you want a friend, you have to be a friend." I don't mean to be simplistic, but I agree with that saying. No one can make a friend for you, and no one else can make you friendly. That is up to you. I personally believe that cultivating friendships is as simple as surrounding yourself with girls who are striving to love and honor God just like you and then making an effort to be kind and friendly to them. You can do it!

Now, that doesn't mean everyone you try to be friends with will become your friend. No worries! Don't get too worked up about that. Just keep on being friendly and I promise you this: you will eventually have friends!

Well, for some reason I don't want to say goodbye to this chapter. It's been so fun connecting and chatting with you about friendship. Let's get together again soon. Like, on the next page!

# *Fourteen*

# Making Your Connections

Let's not sleepwalk through life. . . . Let's keep our eyes
open and be smart. . . . Walk out into the daylight sober,
dressed up in faith, love, and the hope of salvation. . . .
Speak encouraging words to one another. Build up hope
so you'll all be together in this, no one left out, no one
left behind. I know you're already doing this; just keep on
doing it. (1 Thess. 5:6, 8, 11)

con•nect: to come together; to make contact; to closely interact and
communicate

Connections are beautiful opportunities
just waiting to happen.

I walked up to the counter, phone in hand, to make my purchase. I was multitasking. I was on a mission. I had things to do, lists to complete, texts and emails to answer. My plan was for this to be a quick run-into-the-mall moment to grab what I needed and get back on the road to finish my very important to-do list.

The girl behind the checkout counter was sweet and bubbly and seemed ready to strike up a conversation. I set my purchase on the counter and gave her my nicest "I'm in a hurry" smile as my thoughts wandered to the next thing on my list. I tried to be polite as I hurriedly slid my credit card through the machine, hoping that she would notice I needed to move on with my day.

As I scribbled my not-so-legible signature on the screen to complete the transaction, I heard a familiar whisper. *Debbie, this girl is on your to-do list today.*

What!? I was way too busy to stop and chat. Maybe I could come back next week. I tried to shrug off the thought as the girl handed me my receipt. But there it was again. *Debbie, I want you to slow down and take time with this girl.*

I knew what I was hearing was from God. I had heard him whisper those words to me before. So instead of moving on with my day, I paused to purposefully and intentionally take time to look at the girl. And when I did, I immediately noticed something.

Her happy, outgoing personality could not hide the sadness in her eyes. I knew in that moment that God had brought me into this store, to this counter, to make a connection with this girl.

After she finished my transaction, I took time to talk to her. It was obvious that she had been waiting and hoping for someone who would stop and take time to listen. Immediately she began telling me about her life. How she and her husband had recently moved to town. That she had just started her position at the store and did not have any friends.

We chatted a few minutes, and as I started to say goodbye, the thought popped into my mind that I needed to get this girl a latte. I have come to realize that for me, those kinds of thoughts are almost always from God. So in spite of that to-do list that was still screaming for attention, I made my way to the nearest coffee shop, picked up a latte, and brought it back to her. I can still picture her face when I walked back up to her counter and handed her my simple gift. It wasn't big, but it was big to her. Her face lit up with a smile. We chatted a bit more and exchanged phone numbers, and I invited her to the next Sisterhood event at church.

We had made a connection. One that God had planned and I had almost missed out on.

The next day I got a text from her. She told me that she had been very discouraged the day before. Her marriage was a mess, and she was extremely lonely and in need of a friend. She also shared how she had recently heard about our church and had prayed specifically for God to make it possible for her to meet me.

Isn't that amazing! God loves to connect people.

I could have so easily missed that moment if I hadn't been paying attention. Thankfully I didn't. My connection with that girl helped to change her outlook on life and gave her lonely heart the encouragement it needed to go on. She is now back in church, involved and connected with other faith-filled girls. I am so thankful I set aside my schedule and all the things that were vying for my attention that day to stop, look up, and take time to talk with her. I had no idea in that moment that I was actually the answer to her prayer.

One of my favorite stories in the Bible is found in Luke 19 and takes place in the town of Jericho. In that day, Jericho was a thriving community, serving as a destination spot for the wealthy and well-known and as a resting point for those who were making their way to and from the city of Jerusalem. Although wealthy inhabitants lived there, it was also home to a large population of poor and disadvantaged people.

The story begins with these words:

**Jesus entered Jericho and was passing through. (NIV)**

As Jesus made his way into Jericho, he was very likely tired of traveling and weary from teaching and ministering to all the people following him. On that particular day, we can assume there was a large crowd of men, women, and children wanting to see this miracle worker who was passing through town. I can only imagine the pushing and shoving taking place in the streets as hundreds if not thousands of people clamored for position. They were desperate to be noticed, hoping to catch just a glimpse of the man who was known for healing the sick, raising the dead, casting out demons, and calming stormy seas.

In the middle of all that chaos—the pushing and the shoving and the thousands of voices calling out for his attention—was Jesus. He was calmly and purposefully making his way through the crowd, trying to stay on schedule, trying to complete the journey to Jerusalem.

And then, all of a sudden and for no apparent reason, he stopped walking and looked up.

The crowd must have gone crazy with curiosity. "Why is Jesus stopping? What is he going to do? What is he looking at?"

Now I want to introduce you to another character in this story. A man by the name of Zacchaeus. Here are some things we learn about this guy: He was short. He was a chief tax collector. He was wealthy. And he was a notorious sinner with a reputation of being a cheater and a thief. It is obvious that this man was not a good person.

Still, like all the other people that day, this despised and self-ish man had heard that Jesus was coming through town, and he too wanted to see him. But he had a big problem that his money couldn't solve: he was too short to see over the top of the crowd. So he did something that must have looked silly and uncouth to those who noticed. He ran down the street ahead of the crowd and climbed a tree. We can only assume that Zacchaeus must have been desperate. He didn't care what people would think.

Maybe he was tired of the way he was living or just plain tired of living altogether. Sitting up there, peeking through the leaves, he might have been thinking, *If Jesus has the power to heal a blind man, maybe he would have an answer for my miserable life.*

What a moment this must have been. Jesus had every reason in the world to give only a quick nod or a short wave to this man in the tree. But not only did he stop and notice this man of ill repute, he also went a step further. He started a conversation with him.

"Zacchaeus!" Jesus called out. "Come down. I want to come over to your house right now."

Can you imagine that?

Jesus was most likely very tired.

Jesus was crazy-busy.

Jesus had a schedule to keep.

Jesus had people all around him who thought they deserved his attention.

Jesus was under pressure to get things done.

Yet he stopped to take time and connect with this man in his path who was waiting to be seen.

And so Zacchaeus hurriedly climbed out of the tree and took Jesus to his house with "great excitement and joy" (v. 6 NLT). His joyful and enthusiastic response seems to reveal something very important. Even though Zacchaeus may have appeared to be hiding, even though he had a terrible reputation and could have felt unworthy or ashamed to be seen, it is obvious that he desperately wanted to meet Jesus. And he was excited that Jesus had stopped to connect with him.

I want you to think about this. Was it an inconvenience for Jesus to stop and talk to Zacchaeus?

You betcha! He was probably exhausted from walking and tired of meeting people. Jesus had human feelings just like us.

Was it a risk?

Maybe. Remember, Zacchaeus didn't have the best reputation. Verse 7 says "the people were displeased" when they saw Jesus stop and talk to the man who was known as a "notorious sinner."

Did Jesus think Zacchaeus was worth stopping for?

No question he did!

You see, Jesus knew he had the answers for all the questions in Zacchaeus's heart. And in spite of all the reasons or excuses he could have had to just keep on walking, he took time to stop and look up. He interrupted his plans that day and risked his reputation to connect with a little man up in a tree.

I love this story for so many reasons, but especially how it ends.

**Zacchaeus stood before the Lord and said, "I will give half my wealth to the poor, Lord, and if I have cheated people on their taxes, I will give them back four times as much!"**

**Jesus responded, "Salvation has come to this home today."** (vv. 8–9 NLT)

Zacchaeus's life was completely turned around. Because of his encounter with Jesus, he went from stingy to giving, from hurtful to kind, from greedy to generous, from being a lost and lonely man in a tree to being forgiven and set free. And as if that was not enough, everyone in his household was changed by his encounter with Jesus as well. What an incredible story!

---

A few years ago, John and I were boarding a plane to fly overseas for a two-week Bible Seminary tour in Italy, Germany, and Switzerland. We were excited for a break, and we were looking forward to some much-needed rest. As we sat down in our seats, I remember thinking, *I hope the person who will be sitting next to me wants to sleep. I am too tired to talk to anyone.*

Within minutes, a girl about forty years old stopped at our row and said, "Excuse me, my seat is the one next to yours." I let her in, introduced myself, and proceeded to get my stuff all situated for the eight-hour flight ahead—neck pillow, snacks, Bible and notebook in the seat pocket in front of me, carry-on bag tucked away under the seat. Then I took out my earphones and plugged them into my phone. I was all set to go and ready to relax.

As I was putting everything in place, I glanced periodically at my neighbor. Something didn't seem right. She was talking on her cell phone in low tones and seemed very nervous. I couldn't hear everything she was saying, but I did make out the words "afraid" and "I don't know if I can do this" as tears dripped down her face and onto her pants. I sensed as I watched her that it was not by accident she was sitting beside me. God had put her there.

The interesting thing was that John and I had experienced some challenges getting our seats together on the flight. But at the very last minute, the gate agent had called our names. "We were able to work it out," he said. "We moved a couple of people around, and you now have seats next to each other."

Yup, the pieces were coming together in my mind. God had planned this, he wanted me to connect with this girl, and I didn't want to miss what he was going to do. After she ended her call, I put my arm around her shivering body and asked her if she was okay. Her story came tumbling out. Her name was Gina, and she'd just found out the day before that her only brother had passed away suddenly. Her father had called that morning, begging her to come to Germany for the funeral. She immediately called the airlines from her car and was told that she was going to get the last seat on the flight. It was the seat next to me. The phone call I'd overheard was with her dad, and she'd been telling him how she was panicking because of her fear of flying. "I believe God is going to send someone to be with you," he told her.

Gina was a psychologist practicing in Dallas. She had been raised in a Catholic family but had never heard that she could know Jesus personally and that he wanted to know her. I took my Bible out from the seat pocket, and for the next several hours we sat and talked about Jesus. I told her how much he loved her and wanted to be a part of her life. She told me how she had been searching for an answer to life, and she knew in her heart that God had planned for us to connect. Somewhere over the Atlantic Ocean, she prayed the prayer of salvation, asking Jesus to come into her heart and change her life. When she looked up at me after praying, she said with a beautiful smile on her face, "I am not afraid anymore!"

Two years later, when I was in Dallas on a ministry trip, I contacted Gina and we met for lunch. She shared with me that she and her husband were now involved in a Bible-believing church. She was overflowing with joy and thankfulness at the goodness and grace of God in her life, and how he had connected us at just the right time to show her his love and offer her his salvation.

I love that story! It reminds me of how much God delights in connecting us to people who are searching for him, and how he can use a simple conversation to change a life.

But here is the kicker. Opportunities to connect with people don't just happen by coincidence. Listen to what the apostle Paul wrote in Colossians:

> Pray for us, too, that God will give us many opportunities to speak about his mysterious plan concerning Christ. . . . Pray that I will proclaim this message as clearly as I should.
>
> Live wisely among those who are not believers, and make the most of every opportunity. Let your conversation be gracious and attractive so that you will have the right response for everyone. (4:3–6 NLT)

When I read those words from Paul, I am blown away by his desire and commitment to tell people about Jesus. Even though he was in prison being persecuted for what he believed, that didn't stop him! Right there in that dark and dingy cell, he asked for God to give him opportunities to make a difference in the lives of those around him. That is amazing! No matter where he was, in prison or free, he wanted God to open doors for him to share his faith.

Did you happen to notice that little line in the middle of those verses, the one where Paul encourages those to whom he is writing to "make the most of every opportunity"? Paul knew that just because someone had an open door to share about their faith didn't mean they would step out and do it. An opportunity has to be taken for it to be beneficial. The word *opportunity* by definition refers to a favorable circumstance or an opening that allows for something to happen. It represents a choice. And when an opportunity comes to share our faith, there is always a decision to be made. We can take it or leave it. Just like that day in the mall and that morning on the plane, I had a choice. I could take the opportunity or I could miss it or dismiss it.

Purposefully connecting with the people God puts in our path takes faith and effort—faith that God can use us and effort to step out and connect with those people through conversation. That is why Paul goes on to say, "Let your conversation be gracious and attractive so that you will have the right response for everyone" you have an opportunity to connect with. He is reminding us that connecting is pretty simple; it is stepping out and being kind and purposeful in what we do and say. And it almost always means we have to stop what we are doing and put aside our plans and to-do lists to make that connection happen.

Maybe as you read this you are thinking, *Whoa, Debbie, I don't think I have enough faith to share my faith.* Maybe you have never done it before, and you are a bit shy or afraid you won't know what to say. I understand that; there are times when I don't feel as confident as I should. But when I ask God to help me know what to do, he is always ready to give me the confidence and the words to say. Think about this: the greatest preacher in the Bible asked God to help him know what to say. So we are in good company.

What I really want you to understand is this. There are girls all around you waiting for someone to notice them—in your neighborhood, in the grocery store, on a plane, or next to you at work. Girls who desperately need to be encouraged. Girls who need to hear about your faith. Girls who are hoping that you will stop and take the time to look up. God wants to use you to connect with them.

And who knows, you just might be the one who will lead them to Jesus. You might be the connection that will change their life forever!

# *Fifteen*

# Home Where You Belong

You're no longer strangers or outsiders. You *belong* here, with as much right to the name Christian as anyone. God is building a home. He's using us all—irrespective of how we got here—in what he is building. (Eph. 2:19)

**home:** a place surrounded by familiar sounds; a welcoming, relaxed, and safe shelter where one's affections are centered; a place filled with family.

What matters most is not
where you have been
but where you belong!

Whenever I walk through doors of this house, it never fails—my heart feels like it could burst with joy, my spirit feels like dancing, and I am overwhelmed with thankfulness. I love this house. I love the singing and the laughter and the sounds of home saturating the atmosphere and flowing out beyond its walls. It is a place that resounds with worship and praise and displays a grace and unity that come from heaven, welcoming everyone who enters. It is my church, James River Church.

John and I have had the privilege and honor of being the lead pastors of this beautiful and flourishing church family for over twenty-five years. When we pulled into Springfield, Missouri, that October evening in 1991 with our three young children, we had no idea what the journey ahead of us would be like and how God was going to take these two everyday, ordinary people and surprise us beyond our wildest dreams.

When I was twelve years old, I heard God speaking to my heart late one night as I was praying in my makeshift bedroom in the basement of my house. It wasn't a clear, audible voice; it was more like a whispering in my spirit. I knew God was calling me to commit my life to loving and building his church and to lead people to

Jesus. At the time, I didn't have a clue what that would look like. But I made the decision to do everything I could to prepare my heart and life for what he was calling me to do, and I remember being very excited thinking about what the future might look like.

John felt God calling him to be a preacher during his first year of college. After his high school graduation, he had left his home on a farm in Colorado to attend a university in Oklahoma. His plans were to go to law school and become an attorney.

That same fall I moved to Wisconsin along with my parents, who would be serving on staff at a church. I had known for a while that I was in love with John and felt in my heart that he was the guy I would marry, but I was struggling to process how marrying a lawyer lined up with what I knew was God's direction for my life—to be in full-time church ministry. And I didn't want anything, not even a guy I was in love with, to interfere with my obedience to God's will for my life.

Throughout our dating relationship, John had voiced multiple times to me that he had no desire to be in the ministry, especially as a pastor. So that fall I committed to praying for God to show me what to do.

Then one afternoon, two months into John's first semester in college, he called to tell me something that changed both of our lives.

When I heard his voice on the other end of the phone, he sounded very excited. "Debbie, you are not going to believe what happened today. I was in an auditorium with all the pre-law students when a class adviser from the theology department accidently walked in, thinking that was where he was supposed to be, and he began addressing the class. Within minutes, realizing his mistake, he apologized and said, 'If any of you in here want to be fishers of men, come and follow me.'"

John continued on without a breath. "The crazy thing was, I knew immediately he was talking to me. I couldn't stay in my seat, so I got up and followed him out the door." He paused as if to take in what he was about to say. "Debbie, you're not going to believe this either. . . . I'm switching my major. I'm going to be a pastor!"

That moment is embedded in my mind. I remember exactly where I was standing in the kitchen of my parents' home. In one sense, I was blown away by what I heard, and in another, I wasn't surprised at all. God was going before me and putting all the pieces together for the future he had planned for me and for John. Eighteen months after that, we were married and our "build God's church and lead people to Jesus" adventure began.

That fall evening in 1991, when we pulled into Springfield with our U-Haul and three kiddos, I was a bit tentative about the future. We had just walked through a difficult season, and we were tired and discouraged. For over two years we had been the pastors of a home missions church in Kansas City, and it had been very challenging. The truth was, we were exhausted and felt as though we didn't have much to give the people of the new little church we had committed to lead.

James River Church was just eight months old with eighty-five people. But from the first time we had visited the church a few weeks before, it was obvious to us that God's hand was on them for a very special purpose. Our greatest fear in accepting the position was that we would mess up what God wanted to do. So with a prayer that he would somehow use us to continue what he had already begun, we said yes to the board's invitation to serve as their first full-time pastors.

There wasn't anything especially unique about the people who chose to call James River home. But there was definitely something unique about their passion and commitment to build the church. More than anything, they wanted to make their church home a welcoming place to everyone who came through the doors.

And people began to come. That tiny storefront church of eighty-five people began to grow and grow and grow. Over the past twenty-five years of leading this church, we have seen God do more than we could have ever dreamed or imagined possible.

The book of Acts is one of my favorite books in the Bible. If you have never read it, you should. It is the story of the birth of God's church. Listen to this beautiful description of what the church was designed to look like:

> All the believers devoted themselves to the apostles' teaching, and to fellowship, and to sharing in meals (including the Lord's Supper), and to prayer.
>
> A deep sense of awe came over them all, and the apostles performed many miraculous signs and wonders. And all the believers met together in one place and shared everything they had. . . . They worshiped together at the Temple each day, met in homes for the Lord's Supper, and shared their meals with great joy and generosity—all the while praising God and enjoying the goodwill of all the people. And each day the Lord added to their fellowship those who were being saved. (Acts 2:42–44, 46–47 NLT)

Those verses not only are meant to describe what the church was like back then, they are also a picture of what God intends his church to look like today. It is meant to feel like a home, a place filled with joy and blessing. It is meant to be welcoming to all, unified, vibrant, and full of life. People sharing, worshiping, loving, caring, serving, and welcoming others in to hear its life-changing message of hope and salvation.

I am unashamedly passionate about the church. I love everything about it! And I believe it is God's will for everyone who is a follower of Jesus to be a part of it and love it too.

No matter what your past experience has been with church, you need to understand that God never intended it to be quiet, still, solemn, and uninviting. If you think about it, those words together define something that sounds, well, dead. And *dead* is not a word that should describe the church. It was in God's design for his church—no matter the size or the style—to be filled with people brimming with life, energy, laughter, singing and dancing, connection and conversation. It is meant to feel like a home, with an atmosphere where people from every background, status, and circumstance would feel welcome to come through its doors *just as they are*. A place where those who come can grow in their faith and knowledge of God. A place where they can understand that they are a part of a family that loves and accepts one another, and that no matter where they have been, they can belong!

"Why do you care so much about the church?" you might ask.

That's really very simple to answer. Because Jesus did! You see, the church is not a building. That might come as a bit of a surprise to you, maybe because of how you were taught or because you have never understood what it was really meant to be. Maybe you have always thought of churches as buildings hosting a variety of meetings and events. But the church is actually people. It's you and me and anyone else who is seeking to learn more about following Jesus. And wherever followers of Jesus choose to gather to worship him, that is his church. Pretty cool!

Jesus loves his church because he cares about people. The Bible says that the church is the most important entity on planet earth, and he is above it all, loving and leading it.

Listen to what the apostle Paul writes:

> At the center of all this [the universe], Christ rules the church. The church, you see, is not peripheral to the world; the world is peripheral to the church. The church is Christ's body, in which he speaks and acts, by which he fills everything with his presence. (Eph. 1:21–23, brackets mine)

As believers and followers of Jesus, we are a part of the most significant and influential group of people on the planet. Together, through our connected and unified lives, we represent who he is and fill the earth with his presence. What an awesome thought! We are not meant to be an unseen, ineffective, disconnected group of people standing on the outside looking in. The church is intended to be seen, effective, influential, unified in purpose, and at the center of all God is doing across the planet.

It's sad for me as a pastor to watch people who are followers of Jesus separate themselves from the church, his body. Each and every individual believer is purposefully designed to be a vibrant and connected part of the church, active in making it strong, healthy, and whole. Ephesians 4 describes this so beautifully, with a picture of how a healthy church body should function, full of life and love and energy. Each person who calls it home is connected to it, with an understanding that they belong and are a very important part of the family. The apostle Paul said it this way:

> For because of Him the whole body (the church, in all its various parts), closely joined and firmly knit together by the joints and ligaments with which it is supplied, when each part . . . is working properly [in all its functions], grows to full maturity, building itself up in love. (Eph. 4:16 AMP-CE)

I love how those verses paint such a beautiful picture of a healthy body in describing the church. When all the parts are working properly and in order, then we, the body, flourish and are built up. We have the joy of being a part of one another's lives and encouraging each other to grow in faith.

I want you to meet my friend Jennifer, a prominent designer and decorator in our city. About ten years ago, a man she met while working on a design project invited her to come and visit our church. He extended the invitation multiple times and was turned down politely every time. Her continual refusal did not deter him one bit, and one day, when he asked her again, she responded, "Mark, you don't understand. I've been to church.

Why would I want to come to yours? Aren't churches the same wherever you go?"

"I believe you would find this one to be different from anything you have ever experienced," he responded.

Jennifer had been raised in a home that had little to do with God, and she did not know much, if anything, of what it meant to have a relationship with him. From girlhood into her adult life, her only experience with church was attending a place on Sunday that she described as empty and lifeless. The people sang words she didn't understand and seemed to be more concerned with talking about one another than caring for and loving each other, or with (heaven forbid) inviting others who didn't fit in. She would go to church on Sundays because it was the thing to do. She wanted to be close to God, so she kept going and kept searching, but she had no idea why. And that was how her walk with God and her connection to church limped along for years.

When she was twenty-eight years old, she had an experience that changed her view of spiritual things. Late one night she was driving around town with a guy friend who was in a serious battle with drug addiction. In her heart, she knew enough to think that God was the answer to his problems, so she was playing a recording of a pastor preaching about being delivered. At one point in their drive, she came to a stop at an intersection, and the darkness was illuminated by the corner streetlights. As she looked over at her friend, he slowly turned his face toward her, and what she saw froze her heart with terror. The whites of his eyes were bright red, and his pupils and the edges of his eyelids were black. His face was distorted and deformed. As she was trying to take it all in, some raspy, guttural-sounding words that weren't his own came out. The voice yelled at her, "Turn off that &*%$ tape! I don't want to listen to the lies anymore."

In her petrified state, Jennifer remembers thinking, *If there can be this much evil in my car, there must be even greater goodness in the world. God must be bigger.* She started to pray an innocent prayer asking for God to help her. Looking back, she laughs at what she did next, but it was all she knew to do. She started singing the Sunday school song her aunt had taught her: "If the Devil Doesn't Like It, He Can Sit on a Tack." Thankfully she was able to drive her friend home without incident and ended up leaving him and never going back. But the memories of that devilish encounter made her hunger more than ever to know God in a real way.

Years went by, and although that night had affected her deeply, she continued to struggle in knowing how to grow in her relationship with God. Then Mark entered her world and invited her to come to his church. Although at first she wasn't interested, his answers to her questions about church intrigued her. He even told her that she would be welcome just to stand in the back and observe. So one Wednesday night as she was driving home from work, she made the decision to stop at the church and go inside.

Jennifer told me later, "On that night, as I stood in the back of the auditorium and observed the service, my view of God and his church began to change. As I watched the people, listened to the worship, experienced the love and kindness of those around me, and heard the message, my eyes caught a glimpse of all God had to offer. And his desire for me to know and understand who he was and all that he longed for me to be was made clear in the beautiful atmosphere of an alive and healthy church. I felt like I was home."

Within a year, Jennifer, her husband, and their daughter made a commitment to wholeheartedly follow Jesus. Now everything about her life has completely changed. She is growing in her faith, serving in the church, working with women in need, and inviting everyone she can to come into the house that she now calls her home so they too can experience the life and joy that she found there.

"When I would watch the people at James River Church," Jennifer said, "they displayed so much life and energy. They all reminded me of Tigger from *Winnie the Pooh*!"

When she said that to me, I thought, *Yes, that's right.* I loved that! That is truly how the church should look to the world and feel to every guest who walks through its doors for the very first time.

It should be the happiest place on earth, overflowing with joy, resounding with the sounds of laughter and singing, and full of happy people doing life together and making Jesus famous through their connected, unified lives. A place that says to everyone who comes inside, "Welcome home—you belong here!"

# BELIEVING . . .

## *Is for Your Future*

"For I know the plans I have for you," says the LORD.
"They are plans for good and not for disaster,
to give you a future and a hope."
(Jer. 29:11 NLT)

# *Sixteen*

# Dreams Are for Real

God can do anything, you know—far more than you could
ever imagine or guess or request in your wildest dreams!
(Eph. 3:20)

**dream:** a thought or an idea that takes faith to make possible

**hope:** a feeling of expectation and certainty that something will happen
in the future

> Dreams are what realities
> are made of. They are surprises
> waiting to come to life in the future.

remember thinking, *Now that is a ridiculous idea!*
We were sitting in a park one afternoon when something John said made me think he was out of his mind (and the truth is he kind of was). We were just nineteen years old and engaged to be married in a few months, so naturally we were talking and dreaming about our future together when he said, "Someday I believe we will pastor a church of a thousand people."

What was he saying? Was that even possible? It honestly sounded a bit prideful to me.

I had been raised in a pastor's home, and my experience up to that point clouded my ability to see beyond what I viewed as possible. Quite honestly, my faith was diminished by my history, and I ended up judging John's dream by what I had seen in the past. In my human opinion, what he was saying seemed altogether ridiculous and unrealistic. So instead of encouraging him to believe what he was dreaming, I immediately voiced my disapproval and began calculating in my mind just how improbable his dream was. Little did I know that I was speaking directly against God's plan for our lives . . . and our future!

Thankfully God didn't hold my faithless, small thinking against me that afternoon in the park. Instead, he used John's bold dream revelation and our conversation to make me evaluate something very important: was I going to live my life based on what I had seen in the past and viewed as possible, or in believing impossible things that God could see and make happen?

Listen to what this verse says—it's one of my favorites:

> God can do anything, you know—far more than you could ever imagine or guess or request in your wildest dreams! (Eph. 3:20)

I want you to read that again. It is one of the most incredible statements in the Bible.

Just stop and think about those words for a second. *God can do anything, you know.*

In other words, you can't even begin to imagine what God can do in and through your life. Your imagination and my guesses are just a drop in the bucket compared to his ocean of amazing ideas and dreams he has for you and me.

I love that! We cannot even begin to think of or request all of his ideas. He is the ultimate dreamer . . . and the ultimate dream giver.

Do you believe those words are for you? They are! They are not just for missionaries or preachers or monks or your aunt who prays two hours a day and reads all the way through her Bible every year. That verse is for *you*! It is a declaration of what God wants to do through your life. And do you know what it says to me? It tells me that when we are walking with God, our lives are not intended to be boring or ordinary. No sir. They are meant to be filled with God's amazing ideas and unexpected surprises.

The Bible says this about how your "beyond your wildest dreams" life should look:

> This resurrection life you received from God is not a timid, grave-tending life. It's adventurously expectant, greeting God with a childlike "What's next, Papa?" (Rom. 8:15)

That kind of life sounds pretty awesome to me, and very exciting! And it should be. Your spirit is connected to the Spirit of the Creator of the universe, your Heavenly Father. That is a wow! And when the human spirit connects with the divine, creative nature of God's Spirit and his power, then supernatural, out-of-this-world things are going to happen. It's like heavenly fireworks begin to explode with color and life and power when the creativity of almighty God connects to a faith-filled, believing heart.

We should be expecting exciting and awesome things to happen that are beyond our wildest dreams. And why not? He made the universe!

The deal is, I have a choice and so do you. Either we can believe in what God's Word says—that he can do impossible things in and through our lives—or we can stay stuck in the rut of feeling like God would not, could not, or will not do anything like that with our lives. The problem is this: first, that rut is not very exciting, and second, those who live not believing the words of Ephesians 3:20 could quite possibly miss out on the dreams, ideas, and surprises God has planned for them. I don't know about you, but I sure don't want to miss out on any of the amazing, beyond-my-wildest-dreams surprises God has for me . . . and I really wouldn't want you to either.

Throughout history, God has given ridiculous dreams to everyday, ordinary men and women. They had to step out in faith to believe that, with him, what seemed impossible would become possible. Remember Abraham, who was called by God to leave his homeland and everything he was familiar with to journey to an unknown place? Well, he and his wife, Sarah, dreamed of having children. But for years—many years—she was barren and could not conceive. It wasn't until Abraham was seventy-five and Sarah was sixty-five that God finally spoke to Abraham and gave him a promise that their dream of having children would come true. He even promised that their descendants would number the stars.

As the years went by, this dream became more impossible and unrealistic. But when Sarah was ninety years old, she gave birth to a son. Did you catch that? She was *ninety*. Her story shows us that sometimes even dreams from God take time to become reality. Her little guy had one old and happy mama!

How about Joseph, the younger son of Jacob? He had two dreams that revealed to him that one day he would rule over his ten older brothers. When he shared his dreams with his family, his brothers didn't believe him and sold him as a slave. His story reminds us that even when dreams are from God, they aren't always understood by others.

Then there was Esther, the young orphan girl who became a queen. There is actually a book in the Bible named after her. She felt led by God to do something very unrealistic and impossible, and her dream came close to getting her killed. But she chose to believe God in spite of the challenges and danger, and with his help, she was able to rescue an entire nation of people from being annihilated. Esther's story shows us that our dreams almost always include challenges and difficulty.

There are so many stories in the Bible that reveal God connecting with people to bring about his plans, and those plans quite often were looked at as being far beyond possible.

Mary, Jesus' mother, has far and away one of my favorite "dream" stories. Her story is found in the book of Luke. It begins with the angel Gabriel appearing and telling her something absolutely and positively unbelievable—that as an unmarried, young teenage girl, she would conceive, carry, and birth God's Son, the Savior of the world. She would be his mother on earth. Can you imagine that?

Here's how it went down in Luke 1:

> God sent the angel Gabriel to the Galilean village of Nazareth
> to a virgin engaged to be married to a man descended from

David. His name was Joseph, and the virgin's name, Mary. Upon entering, Gabriel greeted her:

> Good morning!
> You're beautiful with God's beauty,
> beautiful inside and out!
> God be with you. (vv. 26–28)

The next verse says that Mary was "thoroughly shaken." In other words, she responded like any normal girl would have. She was petrified. But Gabriel calmed her down and said,

> Mary, you have nothing to fear. God has a surprise for you. (v. 30)

Surprise, indeed—now that has to be one of the greatest understatements in the Bible! Gabriel went on to say,

> You will become pregnant and give birth to a son and call his name Jesus. . . .
>> Mary said to the angel, "But how? I've never slept with a man."
>> The angel answered,
>>
>>> The Holy Spirit will come upon you,
>>>> the power of the Highest hover over you;
>>> Therefore, the child you bring to birth
>>>> will be called Holy, Son of God. . . .
>
> Nothing, you see, is impossible with God.
>> And Mary said, . . .
>>
>>> I'm the Lord's maid, ready to serve.
>> Let it be with me
>>> just as you say. (vv. 31, 34–35, 38)

Can I just say her response amazes me!

I can't help but wonder what Mary was doing the moment Gabriel appeared to her. Was she going about her day, doing laundry or baking bread? Was she sitting quietly under the shade of a tree, humming a worship song? It does seem obvious by her response that she loved God and walked closely with him. And as you probably already know, Mary did become pregnant and give birth to Jesus, the Savior of the world, and she and Joseph raised God's Son.

Mary's example shows us so many things about the way God works and why he reveals his dreams and plans to our hearts. He could have sent Jesus to earth through a number of ways—maybe putting him on Mary's doorstep in a basket or dropping him to earth as a teenager. But God wanted to use a young girl to reveal his divine plan through her.

Here are a few things I want you to notice about Mary and what her story reveals to us about God-given dreams.

*God dreams are for everyday girls.* This story tells us that God loves to use ordinary people to display his glory and power on earth. We don't know a lot about Mary. But what we do know from the story is that she was just a simple, everyday kind of girl. She was young. She was not married. She was from a little village. She wasn't prominent in her community. She wasn't wealthy. She experienced fear at the thought of being called on by God to do something for him. And she needed encouragement, just like you and I do. She was an ordinary girl who was willing to believe God could use her to do something that seemed impossible.

You are no different from Mary. If your life is connected to God's Spirit, he can supernaturally speak to you and give you dreams and ideas that are far beyond your imagination or your own ability. Now, just so you understand, I am not encouraging you to think up things just to be crazy. That's not God's will, and it will get you in trouble. I am talking about your heart and mind being connected to heaven's plan to bring divinely inspired dreams and ideas to life for the purpose of glorifying God.

No one's ever seen or heard anything like this,
Never so much as imagined anything quite like it—
What God has arranged for those who love him.

But *you've* seen and heard it because God by his Spirit has
brought it all out into the open before you. (1 Cor. 2:9–10)

*God, through his Spirit, can and will speak to your heart.* But
his dreams are impossible to hear without his supernatural work
in your life. This is important to remember. If you want to hear
God's Spirit speak to you, you have to be in tune with his language.
Let me just say this: if you are not living in accordance with God's
will in your everyday life, don't expect to understand or even hear
God speaking. It is when you are in tune with him, walking close
to him, and believing in his Word that you will hear him speak to
you. He is looking for people whose hearts are in line with his will
to display his supernatural power through them. They understand
that it is his power alone, working through a yielded and obedient
heart, that makes heaven-birthed dreams possible.

Mary understood that without God, what she was hearing
would never happen. She asked, "How can this be? I have never
been with a man." God-given dreams require us to look to God
as the only source for making them happen. They cannot happen in our own strength and confidence; they need his power to
come alive.

As you already know, the dream John heard God whisper to his
heart before we were married—that someday we would pastor a
church of a thousand people—did end up coming true. And it came
true far beyond what he felt God was speaking to him. When John
spoke those words, my questions reminded me of Mary's. How
could God ever do that, and why would he? Doesn't he know that
we don't have the qualifications for that kind of dream? The truth
is that none of us have the qualifications for what he has planned

to do through our lives. It is only through his power working in us that any God idea or dream is made possible.

What we have seen God do would never have been possible without his power working in us to accomplish his will. The only thing we did was to believe and trust that he was big enough to do it. He and he alone made the dream grow into reality. All the glory is his.

Mary's story reveals several things about divinely inspired dreams.

*Divinely inspired dreams bring glory to God.* The dream God gave Mary would reveal his grace and goodness to all mankind, and it would bring Jesus to earth for our salvation. I love this thought—how every dream God speaks to a human heart is meant to reveal his salvation and bring him glory. Listen to the words in Ephesians 3 again. After Paul says, "God can do anything, you know—far more than you could ever imagine or guess or request in your wildest dreams!" his words explode with praise:

> Glory to God in the church!
> Glory to God in the Messiah, in Jesus!
> Glory down all the generations!
> Glory through all millennia! Oh, yes! (v. 21)

In other words, all dignity, praise, honor, and worship go to God for displaying his supernatural power in and through us on earth.

When God does impossible things through our lives, it reveals who he is to the world and impacts the generations to come with his goodness. It is not for our benefit, although we do benefit from seeing God supernaturally use us. It is ultimately and always for his glory to shine and be revealed.

*Divinely inspired dreams require a submissive, obedient, and faith-filled heart to grow.* Mary wasn't well known. She didn't have a big ministry or a blog with thousands of followers. She was a normal person and had to overcome her own fear and doubt.

Think about it. Ultimately, she had a choice. She could have decided that she did not have what it takes to handle a dream that big. If she hadn't trusted in God to help her, the story could have turned out completely different. She could have said, "I'm not interested in this idea." She could have decided not to believe that God was going to help her. She could have taken matters into her own hands and done something drastic. Mary was human. But she chose to believe that the God who gave her the dream was big enough to make the dream come true. She knew she wasn't enough. She also knew the dream would require hard work and sacrifice. Yet her humble, submissive response reveals her obedient heart:

> I am the Lord's maid, ready to serve. Let it be with me just as you say.

*Divinely inspired dreams come in all different sizes.* The dream God gives you may not seem as big as hearing you are going to be the mother of Jesus, or saving an entire nation, or having a baby at ninety (thank goodness for that!). Some dreams may actually seem small and simple in comparison. But the truth is that no matter how big or small the dream God has given or will give you in the future, it is very important and it is meant to change the world where you live.

In my role as a pastor, girls often share their dreams with me, and I love to hear them. Here are just a few that I have heard recently:

- Christine, a fifty-five-year-old single girl, had a dream to minister to young women with life-challenging issues by providing housing and biblical mentoring. She stepped out in faith and bought a house that was big enough for her to share and now has three girls living with her.
- Robin, at age forty-five, felt God calling her to be a chef and to use her culinary and entrepreneurial skills in the community

as a Christian businesswoman. She left her job after fifteen years to go back to college to start her culinary training.

- Julie, who got saved at age thirty-two, dreamed of speaking to young people about Jesus. She is now coaching softball and shares her faith and prays with the team before each practice and at every game.
- Tammy quit her job as a preschool director to pursue the dream of being in pastoral care ministry. Within months of her stepping out in faith, a door opened for her to volunteer at our church, helping women who are walking through physical and emotional crises.
- Katie is twelve. Her dream was to start an outreach to kids her age. Last year she received permission to launch a weekly Bible study in a classroom at her school, and it grew until the room was overflowing with junior high kids who wanted to talk to her about her faith.

Your dreams and ideas will look different from those of others around you. At some point, each one of these girls had what they thought was an impossible idea cross their mind, and they had to decide to either pray about it or ignore it. And then they had to believe God was speaking to their heart and choose to walk by faith.

Thankfully God doesn't always reveal the scope of the impossible dream he is giving us. Can you imagine if Mary would have understood the ramifications and magnitude of all that Gabriel was telling her?

God knows what we can handle. Honestly, when I look back on that day when John and I were sitting in the park, talking and dreaming about our future, I am so thankful he didn't say, "Someday I believe we will pastor a church of twelve thousand people." I would have thought he had gone crazy (because I did anyway), and who knows, I might have laughed and run away for good!

God is kind enough to reveal only what he knows we are capable of handling. And I for one am thankful for that.

Over and over again in my life, I have seen God take what seemed like an unrealistic, wild, and crazy dream or idea and breathe life into it. Here is just one of my impossible dream stories.

I treasure mornings. I love the quiet and stillness of getting up before everyone else does. It's like my very own space in the day when I can sit with God and share my thoughts and cares with him. But one morning was different. While I was sitting there reading my Bible, a thought came out of nowhere. *Debbie, you need to take a trip to Sydney, Australia.*

Now, that was a bizarre thought. I paused in my Bible reading. Hmm . . . there it was again. I looked up and let the crazy idea sink in. It was like I was hearing a voice in my head speaking to my heart. But why? Why would I even think such a thing? I honestly had no idea, so I ignored it and went back to my reading.

The next day I was back in my spot, curled up in my fuzzy fabric chair by the fireplace, my Bible on my lap and a steaming mug of coffee in hand. As soon as I sat down, there it was again! That crazy thought.

I remember thinking, *That is the strangest idea. Why in the world would I ever want to travel by myself to the other side of the planet?* My knowledge of Sydney was very limited, although I did recall that the well-known Hillsong Church was there, making an impact with their worship music all across the globe.

Now, during that season in my life, I rarely, if ever, traveled alone, except to the grocery store. I did not care to fly and rarely did. Plus a trip to the other side of the planet would be very expensive, and we did not have the money for anything expensive (we had three teenagers!). So that morning, after rehearsing all the negatives, I decided that wherever this idea had come from, it was not meant for me. And I thought that would be the end of the travel-to-Sydney idea.

But it wasn't. No matter how hard I tried to ignore it, day after day, the thought kept coming back to my mind.

It was now October 2004, and I had just recently started working as the women's director at our church. For the past several months, I had been praying for God to give me wisdom to lead the two-thousand-plus women who called James River their church home. Little did I know that the Sydney idea was actually an answer to my prayer, as well as a dream that would require me to believe things far beyond anything I could have imagined possible on my own.

As the weeks went by, I began to think that this strangely persistent idea might actually be God speaking to my heart. I took a faith step and decided that rather than trying to ignore it (that wasn't working anyway), I would start praying for God to show me what to do next.

One thing I have learned over the years is that when I seek God for direction, he almost always uses everyday circumstances to reveal his will, showing me which way to go and what steps I need to take. And on a wintry December evening, that is exactly what happened. That night John and I decided to take some homemade cookies to our new neighbors. They kindly invited us in, and for over an hour we sat and listened to stories about the different places they had lived and traveled. As we got up to leave, the girl of the house turned to me and asked, "Debbie, have you ever been to Sydney, Australia?"

*Oh my goodness. What did she just ask me?* Of all the thousands upon thousands of places in the world, she was asking me about Sydney! I knew in an instant that her words had a divine purpose. So right then and there, with all the faith I could muster, I blurted out the secret that was tucked in the corner of my heart. "No, I haven't, but I kind of think I'm supposed to go there."

As soon as we got in the car, John asked me the question I knew was coming. "Why did you say that you wanted to go to Sydney? I don't see how that could ever happen—it's way too expensive."

Yes, that was true. And I agreed with what he was saying. The idea didn't make sense to me, so why in the world would it to him? But I did notice one thing. I was excited and sensed in my heart that someday this trip was going to happen. So I tucked it away and just kept praying about it.

For the next several weeks, other than while I was praying, I thought very little about my dream. Until one afternoon when I was at lunch with my friend Sandi. As we were leaving the restaurant and walking to her car, she asked me, "Debbie, is there anything on your heart that I can pray with you about?"

Can I just say that I love having faith-filled, dream-believing friends! She was that kind. So without hesitation, I told her what I had been praying about for the past four months. How the idea had gone from a thought to a dream, and now to a prayer and a hope. After listening intently to the story, she boldly stated, "I think you've prayed for this long enough. It's time we figured out how to get you there."

Three months later, on March 10, 2004, Sandi and I, along with my assistant, Karen, were on a plane flying over the ocean! They were sleeping and I was wide awake, praying and wondering where this dream was going to lead me. I had no idea what was about to happen on the plane. It was going to be above and beyond my wildest dreams.

We will get back to this story in the next chapter, I promise!

It is amazing to watch how God takes a dream that he whispers to a believing and praying heart, and connects it to people and events to move it forward. Just think about that in regard to my story. God used our unsaved neighbor and my faith-filled friend Sandi and connected them to my prayers. When you begin to see people and events supernaturally come together, you can always know that God is on the move to bring his plan from heaven down to earth.

It reminds me of that well-known prayer that Jesus prayed. It is known as the Lord's Prayer, and it starts like this:

Our Father Who is in Heaven, hallowed (kept holy) be Your name. Your kingdom come, Your will be done on earth as it is in heaven. (Matt. 6:9–10 AMP-CE)

Do you see that? God's plan is to bring his will to earth. Through people. Through you! Through the thoughts and dreams he puts into your heart. That verse relates not only to world events and world leaders; it's also teaching you and me to pray for his will to be done on this earth through your life and mine.

Before we say goodbye to this chapter, I want to ask you a few questions.

Has God ever given you an idea or a dream? If so, what was it?

Have you seen it start to become a reality yet?

Are you still praying about it, or did you give up on it?

Do you think you are too young or too old for God to speak to you? You're not. Mary was young—very young. Theologians would say she was somewhere around fourteen years old. Sarah was old—very old—when God brought her dream to life. Neither their ages nor their circumstances exempted them from hearing God speak to them and do something impossible through their lives.

What is your dream? I want to challenge you today to start moving forward in your praying to make it happen. Start believing that God can do the impossible through you . . . because if you do, he can.

God can do anything, you know—far more than you could ever imagine or guess or request in your wildest dreams! (Eph. 3:20)

I would love to hear your dream or your dream story. Share it with me at www.debbielindell.com.

# Seventeen

# Rise Up and Shine

Arise, shine, for your light has come,
   and the glory of the Lord rises upon you.
                              Isaiah 60:1 NIV


**rise up:** to get up and to take action

Things will begin to happen
when you start making things happen.

I could hardly believe it was happening. I was on my way to Sydney! That crazy idea, which had started with a simple thought while I sat on my fuzzy chair drinking coffee, was now a reality. And there I was, forty thousand feet over the Pacific Ocean, tucked in between two sleeping beauties—Sandi and Karen—and holding on to the armrests for dear life. I would definitely have qualified as a white-knuckle flyer.

After deciding to start making plans to go, we did a little research and found out that Hillsong Church was hosting a women's conference in March. That sounded like a good time to be there. When we contacted the Hillsong team to let them know we were coming to the conference, they graciously invited us to attend their weekly all-church women's meeting, called Hillsong Women at the time, and offered to provide us with a host during our visit. I was excited about those things, but a bit nervous as well. I had no idea what to expect, and I was still unsure why I was even going.

With my tray table down, I got out my journal, my Bible, and a pen and decided to make the most of these hours of alone time in my seat. I asked God to speak to my heart and reveal to me what he wanted me to see. My prayer went something like this: *God, I have no doubt that you are the one who made this crazy trip happen, and you are the reason I am on this plane. Now I am asking you to please show me why. Amen.*

Let me pause here and say that when you pray for God to speak to your heart, you need to get ready to hear what he says. Listen to what God says to the prophet Jeremiah:

> This is GOD's Message, the God who made earth, made it livable and lasting, known everywhere as GOD: "Call to me and I will answer you. I'll tell you marvelous and wondrous things that you could never figure out on your own." (Jer. 33:2–3)

I love that passage! And that is what I was counting on as I opened my Bible and began to read—that God would answer my prayer and speak to my heart. I was reading that night in the book of Exodus, the second book in the Bible. It is a narrative about the people of Israel who were set free from slavery. The beginning chapters introduce a man named Moses, who was their leader and a central figure in the book.

I was silently reading along to the sound of jet engines humming in the background, when all of a sudden I sensed that God was speaking to me. It was as if he was saying, "Listen up, Debbie. These words are for you."

Here is what I had been reading. In the story, Moses was all alone out in the wilderness, tending his father-in-law's sheep, just minding his own business. He was basically out in the middle of nowhere when, to his amazement, he saw a bush that was on fire but not burning up. He decided to take a closer look, and when he did, he found out that God was up to something.

Two things always come to my mind when I read this story, and they probably did that time as well. One, God loves to surprise us with crazy things. Two, Moses was a very curious person, and I could relate to that. I like to know why, and I probably would have gone over to take a closer look at that burning bush just like he did.

Here is what the Bible tells us about that moment:

When the Lord saw Moses coming to take a closer look, God called to him from the middle of the bush, "Moses! Moses!"

"Here I am!" Moses replied. . . .

"Go, for I am sending you to Pharaoh. You must lead my people Israel out of Egypt."

But Moses protested to God, "Who am I to appear before Pharaoh? Who am I to lead the people of Israel out of Egypt? . . . I'm not very good with words. I never have been, and I'm not now, even though you have spoken to me. I get tongue-tied, and my words get tangled." (Exod. 3:4, 10; 4:10 NLT)

As I read Moses's response to God, I thought, *That's me—that's how I feel.* And right there in my seat, with my seat belt securely fastened, I heard God whisper to me, *You're right, that is you. You are doing the same thing Moses did. I have called you to rise up, and I want you to speak out and lead, but you have been doubting and even complaining. You are not trusting that I can and will provide all you need for what I'm calling you to do.*

I knew God was right (no surprise there!). I had been running scared from what he was calling me to do. I was afraid of failure, afraid of embarrassing myself, and afraid of fumbling the ball. Months before, when the director of our women's department resigned, I had prayed hard for God to bring someone to lead the women. Anyone but me. I had told him I didn't want to do it, I didn't feel adequate, and I was afraid of speaking to audiences of more than four people. But in spite of my protests, God had chosen me and I couldn't get around that. Although I was somewhat excited about my new role, I was also very afraid and insecure about my ability to lead. As I was reading the story of Moses, I knew that God was showing me things in his Word related to my doubt and fear and calling me on the carpet for it. Now it was my turn. How was I going to respond to what he was saying to me?

I wrote in my journal that night about how I was feeling and what I was sensing in my spirit as I prayed and read. My words seemed altogether unbelievable and unrealistic to me. God was saying to my spirit, *I am calling you to speak to thousands. You will stand in front of a full auditorium of women and proclaim my goodness.* What in the world did all that mean? I had no idea. I just remember being very overwhelmed at what I was hearing and writing down.

As I sat in that plane, awake through the entire flight, I thought back to my prayers just a few months earlier, when I had pleaded with God, "Please find someone else to lead the women of our church. Anyone but me." I had told him, "God, you've got the wrong girl. I am not good enough." Finally one afternoon as I was praying and crying out to God on my bed, wadded-up tissues surrounding me, my prayers had changed from "Please don't call on me to lead" to "Here I am; show me what you want me to do." And that is when things began to happen.

In that moment as I spoke those words, my heart changed and I went from dreading the idea of leading the women of our church to feeling excited about it. But I was still trying to understand how God was going to use me to lead when I couldn't even hold a microphone without shaking. So now as I processed those verses from Exodus and what God was saying to me, I was still somewhat confused as to what it all meant. God was going to have to show me what to do next.

When we finally landed in Sydney, our flight was over an hour late, which meant we were going to be late for the Hillsong Women's meeting. We quickly changed in the airport bathroom, washed our hair and dried it under the hand dryers (yes, we did), and drove as fast as we could (which wasn't very fast since we were on the "wrong" side of the road) to meet up with our host at the church.

Walking in, I was surprised to see the auditorium packed full. Bobbie Houston, who pastors Hillsong Church alongside her husband, Brian, was standing at the front getting ready to speak. She paused as our host waved from the back, signaling our arrival. Then as if we had known her for years, she said, "Hey, everyone, our Missouri friends are here. Let's make them feel at home." With that, the roomful of girls began to clap and cheer as we made our way to our seats on the front row, directly facing the podium.

I will never forget what happened next. As we were getting settled in our seats, Pastor Bobbie said, "Okay, girls. Open your Bibles to Exodus chapter 3, to the story where God called a man named Moses to speak and Moses said no."

Can you believe that! Of all the verses and stories in the Bible, she was speaking on the one I had been reading on the plane just hours before. When I heard her say those words, it felt like the room stood still. Everything started to become clear to me. I knew God had brought me here so I would believe that what he was speaking to my heart was true. I knew he would provide everything I needed for whatever he called me to do. If he wanted me to speak, he would give me the confidence and the words to say. If he wanted me to lead, he would give me the wisdom to do it, even if it meant making mistakes in front of thousands of people (which I have done). There was no question in my mind. He was definitely calling me to rise up to a new level of leadership, one that would require me to lay aside my insecurity and go to a new level of submission and dependence on him.

It's easy for me to say that I want to be used by God. The harder part is being brave enough to step out and do what he is calling me to. To trust that he will provide me with the strength and grace and ability to do it. If I'm not careful, the what-if questions can start to take over my mind and cloud my view of God's provision. *What if I'm not good enough? What if I can't do it? What if they think I'm terrible at it? What if I don't have the time, the resources, or even the energy?*

What-ifs are always caused by a "me" perspective, not a God perspective. And whenever I am focused on myself and my ability and my time and my resources, I always come up short. It is when I have my eyes on God as my strength and my source that I am able to walk with confidence, secure in knowing that he will provide me with everything I could possibly need to accomplish his will.

Philippians 4:13 is the perfect verse to help us keep our eyes focused right:

**I can do everything through Christ, who gives me strength. (NLT)**

God is the ultimate and never-ending source of everything we need!

I can't help thinking that you might be in a situation where you are doubting your ability. Maybe God has given you an idea, and you know he is calling you to rise up and do something for him. And maybe, just like me and Moses, you have tried to convince God that he has picked the wrong person for the job. You know you're running from what he is calling you to do because you're afraid of what it will take and that you aren't good enough. You are frantically pleading with God to provide a different solution or to find someone besides you for the job. Can I suggest that you change your pleading to praying, "Here I am, God; I'll do whatever you call me to do"?

I can tell you from my own experience that changing the way you pray will completely change your perspective toward what God is calling you to do. The problem may be that you are just too afraid of what you're going to hear. Stop being afraid of what God might say to you! He is not going to ask you to do more than you can handle, and he will never leave you to do it alone.

That trip to Sydney continued to reveal things to my heart that were beyond my imagination and most definitely beyond my ability. When I walked into the Colour Women's Conference, God opened my eyes to see what he had planned for me and the girls of James River in the future. As I looked across that auditorium filled with thousands of women of all ages and backgrounds, gathered together for the purpose of connecting, having fun, worshiping God, and growing in their faith, I was blown away. All the pieces came together in my mind. I knew that God was calling me to rise up and lead the girls of our church to believe bigger things, to equip and teach them to be faith-filled, and then to open the doors of our church home to gather and welcome every girl to come and be a part of what God was going to do.

That was twelve years ago. When I came home, I was a different person. God had changed my heart, and I was excited and energized about what he had planned. He had opened my eyes to see things that I never could have dreamed possible on my own.

As I stepped out by faith and believed in what he was calling me to do, a host of faith-filled girls came alongside me. Working together and with God's help, we launched the Designed for Life Women's Conference that next year and the Designed Sisterhood ministry a few years later. And by his amazing grace, this past year we hosted over eight thousand girls at the conference.

I am in awe of God and his goodness. As I trusted him, he took my hand and gave me everything I needed to accomplish his will. Through that tiny seed of a dream on my prayer chair one morning, thousands of girls have heard about Jesus, have been encouraged in their faith, and have become "sisterhood" friends forever. My heart is different, our ministry looks different, and the church has been strengthened as the girls (and guys) of our church family have embraced what God has called us to do. And he gets all the glory!

Here is what I want you to understand. God is looking for people who are willing to say yes to him. People who will step out in faith and respond to his leading. It isn't the size of the task or dream that matters, because if the dream is from God, it is significant no matter how big or small. The most important thing is this—that you are listening for God's voice and willing to rise up and respond when he calls on you.

A couple years ago, I was in a checkout line at the grocery store one morning. In front of me was a mother with her two young children. I thought she looked tired and stressed as she set her single purchase on the conveyor belt—a dozen confetti-sprinkled cupcakes from the bakery. As I watched her digging in her purse for her wallet, I heard a whisper. *Debbie, I want you to pay for those cupcakes.*

I remember thinking, *God, is that really you? I'm sure she can probably manage to pay for her own cupcakes. And besides, what if it embarrasses or upsets her?*

I had only a minute to make my decision, not much time to debate God on this one. Would I rise up or shrink back? As I paused to deal with my what-ifs, it was as though I could feel God nudging me from behind, urging me gently to respond to his whisper. I stepped around her quietly, slid my credit card through the machine, and slipped back behind her before she even noticed what I had done. The checker handed her a bag with the cupcakes in it and told her they had been paid for by the lady behind her.

The mom smiled politely, whispered a soft "thank you," and walked away. At the time, I did not realize she attended our church. A year later I received this note from her:

*Dear Debbie,*

*You don't know me personally, but a year ago you paid for my daughter's birthday cupcakes at the grocery store.*

*On that morning, me and my two kiddos, Nicklaus and Lola, were running late for school. As I loaded them into the car, I remembered that it was Lola's day to bring cupcakes for her class birthday party. I started to stress out because I knew we only had 13 cents in our checking account. I had no money or credit cards in my wallet because we were trying to get out of debt. My mama panic was escalating as I backed out of the driveway. Trying to pretend like nothing was amiss, I had the kids pray for their day, and I silently asked God what to do. In that moment, I heard him say, "I want you to go ahead and stop at the store and pick up cupcakes."*

*As I walked into the store, in my head I was shouting at God, "Why am I here? I can't pay for cupcakes. I don't have any money!" I had absolutely no idea what I was going to do. At the checkout, I looked up and you were right next to us in line. As I was desperately trying to think up a solution, to my surprise, the checker just handed me my bag of cupcakes and told me they had been paid for by you!*

*Thank you, Debbie! Since that day in the grocery store, our lives have changed and our finances have completely turned around. I am eternally grateful that you listened to God that morning. You were an angel sent by him to help place our family on the path that he has laid out before us—to trust him always and completely with everything!*

> *Much love and hugs,*
> *Dana*

Thankfully I didn't let my what-ifs keep me from responding by faith to God's voice. I listened and responded to his leading that day.

I want to leave you with a few practical thoughts about listening and responding to God's leading in your life.

Hearing from God isn't mysterious; it's personal. If you walk close to him, you will hear him speaking to you.

When God calls you to do something for him, you can know that he will provide you with the faith you need to move forward—you just have to take the first step.

Whether the task seems big or small, it is always important. If you don't respond, who will? You might miss out on blessing a mom with cupcakes and a whole lot more.

Whenever God calls you to do something for him, Satan will be right there to discourage you from doing it every single time! Don't listen to him.

When you rely on yourself, you will always come up short. When you rely on God, you will always have everything you need for what he is asking you to do.

God wants to take you places you never dreamed of going and use you in ways you never imagined possible. But you will have to believe that to see it happen. God works through us to accomplish his will, but we still have to work to see it come to be.

Rise-up opportunities come in all different shapes and sizes. Speaking on a platform and leading a ministry may never be something you are called to do. But as you listen for God's voice, you will hear him whisper and call you to do things that bring him just as much glory! Amen!

# *Eighteen*

## The Sisterhood Revolution Is Now

Walk out of the gates. Get going!
   Get the road ready for the people.
Build the highway. Get at it!
   Clear the debris,
   hoist high a flag, a signal to all peoples! . . .
   "Tell daughter Zion, 'Look! Your Savior comes,
Ready to do what he said he'd do
   prepared to complete what he promised.'"

Isaiah 62:10–12

rev•o•lu•tion: a change in one's thinking; an organized movement;
a gathering of people who desire to influence the world

United we love each other;
together we change the world.

My eyes were wide, taking it all in. Four weeks earlier, I wouldn't have dreamed that this is where I would be. I was going on another surprise adventure with God. Intense emotion flooded my soul as the oversized van made its way through the dingy tunnel that would take me and my traveling companions to another world. It was a world I didn't know existed. Looking out the window, I saw a very sickly and half-dressed woman holding a naked little boy, maybe two years old. The dirt and grime covering his face and body made it difficult to tell. I had never seen anything like it—only on television, and that, I had already decided, was not the same.

The night before, we had stayed in a hotel—or what they called a hotel—two blocks from the border crossing. When we had pulled up to the door of the two-story building, rain was coming down by the bucketload, and it seemed as though the huge bolts of lightning were aiming at us as we sprinted from the safety of the van into the hotel lobby.

The lobby was a very small room, with chipped and cracking marble floors, revealing to me that at some time in its past this now sad little building had been a place of beauty. But not anymore. To our left was a marble staircase that had, for the time being, turned into a cascading waterfall. The holes in the walls and roof welcomed the buckets of rain. I am not easily frightened (except of heights, that is), but this was the creepiest place I had ever seen in my life.

My friend Tami and I were escorted up the watery staircase to our room on the second floor. It contained two metal twin bed frames holding very worn and dirty mattresses, an old broken-down chest of drawers, and a small wooden chair. As we sat on the beds assessing our sleeping situation for the night, flashes of lightning and loud crashes of thunder filled our room. We both knew sleep would not come easy.

For dinner that night we met in the hotel restaurant (I say that loosely) on the first floor next to the lobby. I remember thinking, *This place looks like a scary movie set.* Ten unmatched wooden tables and chairs were scattered around the room, which was dimly lit by two small lightbulbs hanging from black cords. Our group of ten travelers pulled a few of the tables together under one of the lightbulbs and sat down.

There was only one other table with seated guests—a middle-aged man who sat between two barely dressed, empty-eyed teenage girls, both with heavy, dark makeup and bright red lips. The overweight man had unkempt, stringy, dyed black hair, and his face was covered with multiple scars from wounds that had long since healed without proper medical care. He seemed oblivious to us, and in between shoveling oversized bites of food into his mouth, he would make out with one of the girls beside him, then the other. Looking at him made me physically ill. Everything within me wanted to scream and go rescue those precious young girls, but all I could do was pray.

Back in our room, Tami and I couldn't get the scar-faced man and the girls out of our minds. Even though we had decided it might be wise to wedge the little wooden chair under the doorknob and keep our street clothes on, we still felt very vulnerable. As I closed my eyes, I thought, *We're not even in Haiti yet.*

It had been just ten days before that I was praying as I drove the twenty-five-mile trip home from a friend's baby shower. We were less than four weeks away from the opening night of our Designed for Life Women's Conference, and I had this feeling that God wanted me to step out in faith again to believe something big, but I didn't know what it was. I had been praying for several weeks about the conference, as it was growing rapidly and gaining strength from the very first event, when 347 courageous James River Church girls stepped out in faith with me. Now, four years later, we anticipated over two thousand girls would gather for this event.

The team and I could feel God's hand of blessing and favor as we prepared and planned. It was obvious to us that the influence of the conference was expanding, as women of all ages and walks of life—from the church, the community, and the state—were beginning to talk about how it was impacting their lives each year. It was a privilege to strengthen, encourage, and inspire each and every girl who came.

But even though the conference was growing, I could not stop thinking something was missing. I felt that God was telling me there was more, and I was beginning to feel desperate to know what it was. That day in the car, I told God, "If you want to do something new at the conference this year, I need to let you know you're running out of time!" It is so funny what we tell God, isn't it? Like he didn't know that!

I remember exactly where I was on the road that day when my cell phone rang. It was a friend who had been praying with me. When I heard her voice on the other end of the phone, I could tell she had something exciting to say. That very day she had connected with someone from a ministry called One Child Matters, a child sponsorship organization that had started in India fifty years before. As she told me the little bit she knew about the program, I could sense in my spirit that what I was hearing was a direct answer to my prayer.

Within minutes of hanging up from that call, I was on the phone with one of the directors of the program. He told me about the need in Haiti and the trip they were about to take and asked me if I would want to go. I knew it was God.

So there I was with the team, getting ready to travel across the border into what is known as the poorest country in the Western Hemisphere. I had no idea that what lay beyond that dividing wall would be worse than what I had experienced the night before at the hotel. Once on the other side, I would feel like I had been transported to another planet, one that was altogether different from anything I had ever seen. A place that smelled of urine; where trash is not trash; where completely naked, hungry toddlers and mangy dogs wander side by side on filthy streets; where families live in paper shacks and sleep on dirt; where voodoo is the national, practiced religion; and where people do unheard of and unnatural things in the name of that religion. Haiti is a place where only 30 percent of the population has any income, where crime is rampant, and where life has very little meaning to most who live there. It is a place that is desperate for change and desperate for Jesus.

We were in the country for only eight hours that day because it was too dangerous to stay overnight in the areas we were visiting. But it took less than five minutes for me to know that I would do whatever I could to make a difference in the lives of the people there.

When I think about that day, my mind floods with the memories. I remember walking along a narrow path on the outskirts of a village and through the dense jungle brush, hearing the distinctive, tender cry of a newborn baby. As our little team came to a small clearing, we saw a one-room shanty with a weary mother standing out front holding her newborn baby. She was beautiful. Her gorgeous brown eyes smiled and her dark skin glowed from perspiration as she handed me—a stranger—her tiny, naked baby.

We could not communicate with words, but her expression was enough to welcome me inside her home. On the floor in the corner was her dying father. I'll never forget that moment. As I knelt next to him to pray, with his tiny granddaughter in my arms and his daughter gazing at my very white face, my eyes welled with tears and I thought, *So this is what Jesus must have felt like when he was overwhelmed by all the needs of people.* He must have felt the same things I was feeling. I wanted to do more. I wanted to bring them home. I wanted to change their lives. I wanted to give them hope. I wanted to bring them salvation. This new mother represented so many people who were in need of someone to say, "I will help. I will lift my voice to make a difference for you."

When we came home, we were different. I was different. That one day not only changed my life personally but also changed the direction of the women's conference and the lives of thousands of children and families. I decided to use whatever influence God had given me through the conference to motivate that army of girls to help bring change and Jesus to those people. To date, we have helped to establish fifteen One Child Matters projects, sponsoring over three thousand individual children in the countries of Haiti and Ethiopia.

As I think back to that Sunday and the phone call I received, I wonder what would have happened if I had let fear govern my decision. What if I had said it would be too hard to go, or I didn't have enough time to prepare? What if I had said no? An opportunity can come once and you can miss it. To not miss those God-sent opportunities, you have to live ready, you have to be willing, and you have to know when to say yes!

Remember Esther? She stepped out in faith to save her people from annihilation. She was an orphan who, as a young girl, was forced from the safety of her cousin's home to become a mistress in the palace of the king of Persia. From there, this seemingly insignificant social outcast was chosen by the king to become his queen. The Bible says that Esther was born "for such a time as this" (Esther 4:14 NIV). Out of an obscure and unknown existence, God chose her to be a queen, to influence a government, and to affect the decisions of powerful leaders. Through heaven's divine plan, she found herself with an opportunity that was beyond anything she could have imagined possible.

Esther had a choice. She didn't have to respond. But she did. Through her prayers, her voice, and her determination to make the most of her opportunity, God used her to bring massive change and rescue an entire nation from being destroyed. She took the opportunity and decided to use her life to make something happen!

Albert Einstein said, "Nothing happens until something moves."[1] How true. And one person is all it takes to start a movement and bring change. You can start a revolution, my friend! But before that can happen, you may have to change first. Your thinking may have to change. You may need a revolution in your heart and mind first—a revolution of faith to believe that God can use you.

In between services at church this past Sunday, my assistant and I met with a girl named Sherry. She is in her midthirties, is nicely dressed and sharp, has a good job, and is involved in church. As she walked into the room where we were meeting, her shoulders sagged and her chin nearly touched her chest. When I greeted her, her apprehensive gaze met mine, and it was obvious her insecurity and feelings of self-deprecation were like weights on her head.

Although she desired to do things for God, this precious and beautiful girl was trapped and weighed down by the lies of Satan. With just a few minutes of conversation behind us, it was apparent to me that she viewed herself as having little to give to the world or to be used by God. As we talked, I thought, *Wow, this girl has so much to offer. If only she believed she did.*

Within the first few minutes of our conversation, I asked, "Sherry, were you afraid to come in here and talk to us today?" She hung her head again and then nodded slowly. I took her hand, gently pulled her over to the full-length mirror in the room, and asked her to look at herself. It took her several minutes before she could even lift her head to face the image in the mirror. When she finally did, it was with sadness and embarrassment.

I took her face in my hands and said, "Sherry, until you believe that God made you just the way he wanted you to be and that he thinks your body, your personality, and your gifts are exactly what he designed them to be, you will not be able to live the life he intended you to live." I proceeded to tell her how much she had to give, and how her compassion and love for hurting people and her desire to help those around her came through in spite of her insecurity. I told her that until she chose to believe what her Creator says about her and changed how she viewed herself, she would be trapped, focusing only on herself and how others viewed her.

That is the interesting thing about insecurity. It entraps you in your own self-thinking. Self-centered thinking is the enemy of living a revolutionary life for God. Instead of looking around at how you can make things happen to bring his love and light to earth, you are focused on yourself and on how others view you. Consequently, opportunities to be used by God and make a difference for him are missed, your life is minimized, and Satan scores a victory. But it doesn't have to be that way. There is a way to get victory over your insecurity—by believing what God says about you.

Sherry acknowledged her feelings that day and listened to the counsel she was given. We prayed together, and when she walked out the door, she was grinning from ear to ear and looked nearly three inches taller! Now, most likely our conversation and prayer didn't completely zap her feelings of insecurity forever. They will probably surface again. I still face the insecurity battle at times too. And when I do, I have to go back to what I know to be true and remind myself of what God says about me.

The truth is God cannot change the world through you or me until we think more about the world than what the world thinks of us. And that can only happen when there is a revolution in your heart and mind!

*Revolution* is such a powerful word. It signifies a passion and desire to see change in someone's thinking or in the way things have been. It carries a message of transformation, hope, strength, and resolve. It represents a life determined and committed to make things better. A person who is willing to fight for what they believe is right, no matter the cost, and one who makes the most of every opportunity they are given.

Throughout the course of history, the world has witnessed thousands of revolutions to bring change for good. They began with one person who, with passion and a determination to make things different, lifted their voice to say "enough is enough" regarding the circumstances around them. Most of them were everyday, ordinary people willing to step out when opportunity came and then stand up and make a difference.

God is inviting us to be a part of the revolution that he began through his Son Jesus:

> Walk out of the gates. Get going!
>   Get the road ready for the people.
> Build the highway. Get at it!
>   Clear the debris,
>   hoist high a flag, a signal to all peoples! . . .
>   "Tell daughter Zion, 'Look! Your Savior comes,
> Ready to do what he said he'd do,
>   prepared to complete what he promised.'"
>   (Isa. 62:10–12)

God wants you to be a part of what he is doing across the earth. He is bringing together his daughters from near and far—those who have been in bondage, abused, and hurt but are now set free; those who have been scattered and lost but are now gathered and found. An army of girls of every age, hand and hand, marching as one.

God invites you to be a part of what he is doing and to bring a revolution to the situations that surround you. I am not talking about being defiant or militant. I am talking about being fully dedicated and committed to his will, watching him use your life, your determination, and your faith to bring supernatural change to the world around you. God is calling you to pick up his flag and start waving it!

It's our flag—the flag of heaven! It represents redemption, hope, freedom, and salvation. Pick it up, hold it high, don't be ashamed, don't be afraid. Shout for joy, for victory is coming in Jesus' name!

And as you raise it, you will see that you are not alone. There is a sisterhood of faith-filled girls surrounding you, and we all belong together! We are standing tall and proclaiming what we believe with confidence and strength, that we are not ashamed of the gospel:

It's news [we are] most proud to proclaim, this extraordinary Message of God's powerful plan to rescue everyone who trusts him. (Rom. 1:16, brackets mine)

What is that I hear? Listen! It is a mighty army of women of all ages and all walks of life.

Thousands upon thousands of beautiful girls who are gathering across the land and uniting as one.

Together, with one heart, one voice, and one mission, they are marching side by side, cheering each other on in this journey of life. They are walking hand in hand and offering their collective lives— their time, their talents, and their resources—to bring change . . . a heaven-breathed revolution of the hope of Jesus to the world.

Put your boots on, sweet girl! Stand up, stand out, and be committed to what you believe. Then step out and do what God has called you to do . . . and let the sisterhood revolution begin!

Do you hear the daughters sing?
Singing the song of the redeemed?
It's a song that proclaims freedom

And salvation to the world.
When the beating of our hearts
Echoes the song that angels sing,
We will shout it out as one:
Jesus our Savior reigns!

You are a part of this army of daughters, you are a part of the sisterhood revolution, and you are a part of the song. So raise your flag high and sing, baby, sing!

# A NOTE
## This Is Not the End

That's why we live with such good cheer. You won't see us drooping our heads or dragging our feet! Cramped conditions here don't get us down. They only remind us of the spacious living conditions ahead. It's what we trust in but don't yet see that keeps us going. (2 Cor. 5:6–7)

**jour•ney:** traveling from one place to another

Life is not a destination.

It's our journey home.

You made it to the end! Or did you skip to this page? If you did, I don't mind. I might have done that too. But I have a surprise for you—this is not goodbye. It's just the end of my words for now. After the last page is turned, life and our journey on earth will continue on in the setting where God has positioned us.

My greatest hope and prayer is that somehow, by God's grace touching my simple words in the pages you read, you have gained supernatural strength and wisdom and confidence for your life today and for the days ahead of you. And that your faith to believe in God's Word and his supernatural power at work in your heart and life has been strengthened.

I promise I will never stop praying for you—praying that you will keep growing deeper in your love for and commitment to follow Jesus and in the knowledge of his love for you. I pray that someday, if we haven't already met, we will meet face-to-face—if not on this planet, then in our new home with Jesus in heaven. I will invite you over to my place for coffee (yes, coffee will be in heaven—I'm pretty sure Chris Caine told me so).

My emotions are mixed as I write these last few pages to you. I'm excited to be finished with the book and sad to see it end. It's been quite an adventure. Two weeks after I signed the contract with the publisher to write this book, I found out I had breast cancer, and my journey through the most difficult year of my life began. In many ways, you were there with me. Even though this book is not the story of my cancer journey, what God did in me through those months of trial is sprinkled throughout these pages. I am a different person. I'm more committed than ever to do what God calls me to do, to go wherever he sends me, and to use my life and the remainder of my time on this earth to shine the light of the gospel to everyone around me.

It's late now, and I am sitting in the dark, typing to you on my phone. I'm humming an old church song: "When we all get to heaven, what a day of rejoicing that will be! When we all see Jesus, we'll sing and shout the victory!" I'm thinking about the world we live in (I'm a multitasker), and it is nothing like the world my precious grandma Alice was a part of. This past Sunday I wore my skinny jeans with the torn knees to church and thought, *If my Norwegian grandma would have caught me wearing these to church, she would have said, "Uff da!"* And she would have wanted to mend them for me on the spot.

My jeans, and whatever else I wear to church these days, are insignificant compared to the change in the climate and the massive decline of right and wrong in our world. Immorality and sin abound. Entertainment is primarily governed by sex and filth. And then there are the atrocities we seem to hear about daily—sex trafficking, pornography, violence, and terrorist plots are a part of everyday life. Women and children are being abused daily, in *my* city, and many are forced to hide in shelters from predators they know and fear.

Yes, the world is different. It has declined dramatically in my lifetime, and it is heartbreaking. But here is the good news! Where sin increases and abounds, grace—God's unmerited favor—surpasses it, increases more, and super abounds (see Rom. 5:20).

We have this assurance and we believe God is with us. He has not relinquished his throne. He has not left us alone to navigate the challenges that surround us. And he is calling us all to a new level of faith—to believe what we believe and live it out loud for all the world to see.

> Since God assured us, "I'll never let you down, never walk off and leave you," we can boldly quote,
>
>> God is there, ready to help;
>> I'm fearless no matter what.
>> Who or what can get to me? . . .
>
> There should be a consistency that runs through us all. For Jesus doesn't change—yesterday, today, tomorrow, he's always totally himself. (Heb. 13:5–6, 8)

Be strong, sweet girl. Be bold. Be confident! I promise that when you believe in the truth of God's Word and what he says about you, you will be different.

Your life will have present and eternal meaning and purpose.

You will see God work through you.

You will see real miracles happen.

And the world around you will know that there is a girl who loves God with all her heart, and she not only believes in him but is also living what she believes.

> So reach out and welcome one another to God's glory. Jesus did it; now *you* do it. . . . Just think of all the Scriptures that will come true in what we do! (Rom. 15:7–8)

We will join together—girls of all ages, from all nations, all backgrounds, all histories, and all colors and races—giving God hearty and joyful praise! And we will all celebrate and believe God together (see Rom. 15:8–11).

May the God of green hope fill you up with joy, fill you up with peace, so that your believing lives, filled with the life-giving energy of the Holy Spirit, will brim over with hope! (v. 13)

See you again soon at our favorite café. Until then, keep believing, my friend.

With love,
Debbie

# NOTES

### Chapter 2   Your Reflection Is Beautiful

1. Robin F. Goodman, quoted in "I'm 12 and My Identity Is Online. What?" *Online Journal of Christian Communication and Culture*, December 6, 2011, http://www.ojccc.org/2011/12/im-12-and-my-identity-is-online-what.

### Chapter 6   Prayer—a Difference Maker

1. Dietrich Bonhoeffer, *The Cost of Discipleship* (New York: Touchstone, 1995), 163.

### Chapter 12   Big Girls Do Cry

1. Lizette Borreli, "Why Do We Cry? The Three Different Types of Tears and Their Physiology," *Medical Daily*, May 1, 2015, http://www.medicaldaily.com/pulse/why-do-we-cry-three-different-types-tears-and-their-physiology-331708.

### Chapter 18   The Sisterhood Revolution Is Now

1. Albert Einstein, "Inspirational Quotes," En-Theos, https://www.entheos.com/quotes/by_teacher/Albert%20Einstein/page/3.

**Debbie Lindell** serves alongside her husband, John, Lead Pastor of James River Church in Springfield, Missouri. In 2003, Debbie launched the Designed for Life Women's Conference, which today draws 10,000 women annually from across the nation and around the world. As a dynamic leader and speaker, she has a passion to see women of all ages embrace their unique design, understand their purpose, and connect to one another through life-giving sisterhood. Learn more at DebbieLindell.com.

**Susy Flory** is a *New York Times* bestselling coauthor and the author of several other books. Her writing has been featured in *Focus on the Family*, *Guideposts*, and *Today's Christian Woman*. She lives in the San Francisco Bay area with her family.

# LET'S STAY CONNECTED!

Sisterhood is a gift from heaven. It represents the beauty of life-giving relationships and the immense influence, power, and creativity women have when they are united in friendship, heart, and purpose.

The sisterhood that is uniting across the earth is embracing, colorful, and multifaceted—an intricate and varied network of women young and old, near and far, from every season of life. Each one adds strength and vibrancy to the whole through her unique design. This rising movement of sisterhood is beautiful and brave, graceful and strong—women ready and willing to use their collective lives to stand up for righteousness and shine the light of salvation to the world around them.

**Together we are stronger!**

**VISIT ME AT DEBBIELINDELL.COM.**

- Be encouraged, strengthened, and inspired through the *Designed Sisterhood* blog.
- Share "She Believes" testimonies and hear stories from other women just like you.
- Join me for a book study of *She Believes*.
- Share your prayer requests and receive support for the season you are walking through.
- Find information on the Designed for Life Women's Conference, Designed Sisterhood events, and my speaking schedule.
- Follow me: 📘 and 🐦 #shebelievesbook

**UNITED WE LOVE
EACH OTHER . . .
TOGETHER WE
CHANGE THE WORLD!**

# DESIGNED FOR LIFE WOMEN'S CONFERENCE

The Designed for Life Women's Conference was launched in 2003 and is hosted by Pastor Debbie Lindell and a team of amazing people who make it possible. The vision emanates from the Designed Sisterhood ministry of James River Church with the message that every woman is beautifully and uniquely designed by her Heavenly Father for an incredible purpose.

The Designed for Life experience is:

• **An ever-expanding sisterhood movement—women of all ages, from every season and walk of life.**

• **A gathering of thousands of women coming together to be refreshed, encouraged, and strengthened to live life beautifully and purposefully.**

• **Two fantastic days and nights filled with spectacular production, life-giving teaching, and dynamic worship.**

• **An inviting and welcoming atmosphere filled with joy, laughter, and surprises.**

• **More than an event—we unite in friendship, heart, and purpose to use our collective lives, talents, and resources to influence our homes, our neighborhoods, our communities, and the world.**

• **A platform for bringing hope and justice to hurting and marginalized women and children in our communities and beyond through the Project 12 initiative. You can join the sisterhood in praying at noon every day for this cause— #notonourwatch campaign.**

Designed for Life Conference – Every Fall – Springfield, Missouri, USA

FOR MORE INFORMATION AND TO REGISTER, VISIT WWW.DESIGNEDFORLIFE.ORG

James River Church | Springfield, Missouri

# WELCOME HOME TO JAMES RIVER CHURCH

John and Debbie Lindell have been the lead pastors of James River Church since 1991. With a passion to share the message of the gospel and see people find hope and abundant life through knowing and following Jesus, we believe the church was designed to be a place where everyone feels welcomed and at home—a place that:

- **Reveals God's love to every human heart.**
- **Presents the gospel through biblical teaching and personal relationships.**
- **Faith grows, prayer is heard, and miracles happen in the lives of people.**
- **Shines the light of salvation in our community and around the world.**
- **Is full of life and filled with the sounds of heaven—joy, laughter, and singing.**
- **Says to all who enter, "Welcome home, you belong here!"**

If you do not have a church home or would like to know more about following Jesus, we would welcome you to join us at one of our campuses, listen to our podcast, or connect with us online at www.jamesriver.org.

---

"You're no longer wandering exiles. This kingdom of faith is now your home country. You're no longer strangers or outsiders. You *belong* here. . . . God is building a home. He's using us all—irrespective of how we got here—in what he is building."
—**Ephesians 2:19–21**